ADVERTISING

OPPOSING VIEWPOINTS®

Other Books of Related Interest

ADVERTISING

OPPOSING VIEWPOINTS®

Laura K. Egendorf, *Book Editor*

Bruce Glassman, *Vice President*
Bonnie Szumski, *Publisher*
Helen Cothran, *Managing Editor*

OPPOSING
VIEWPOINTS®
SERIES

GREENHAVEN PRESS

An imprint of Thomson Gale, a part of The Thomson Corporation

THOMSON
™
GALE

Detroit • New York • San Francisco • San Diego • New Haven, Conn.
Waterville, Maine • London • Munich

For more information, contact
Greenhaven Press
27500 Drake Rd.
Farmington Hills, MI 48331-3535
Or you can visit our Internet site at http://www.gale.com

Cover credit: © Jerzy Dabrowski/DPA/Landov

LIBRARY OF CONGRESS CATALOGING-IN-PUBLICATION DATA
Advertising / Laura K. Egendorf, book editor.
p. cm. — (Opposing viewpoints series)
Includes bibliographical references and index.
ISBN 0-7377-3226-1 (lib. : alk. paper) — ISBN 0-7377-3228-8 (pbk. : alk. paper)
1. Advertising—Moral and ethical aspects—United States. 2. Sex in advertising—United States. 3. Advertising—Political—United States. I. Egendorf, Laura K., 1973– . II. Opposing viewpoints series (Unnumbered)
HF5831.A34 2006
659.1—dc22   2005040262

"Congress shall make
no law...abridging the
freedom of speech, or of
the press."

First Amendment to the U.S. Constitution

The basic foundation of our democracy is the First
Amendment guarantee of freedom of expression.
The Opposing Viewpoints Series is dedicated to the
concept of this basic freedom and the idea that it is
more important to practice it than to enshrine it.

Contents

Why Consider Opposing Viewpoints?

"The only way in which a human being can make some approach to knowing the whole of a subject is by hearing what can be said about it by persons of every variety of opinion and studying all modes in which it can be looked at by every character of mind. No wise man ever acquired his wisdom in any mode but this."

John Stuart Mill

In our media-intensive culture it is not difficult to find differing opinions. Thousands of newspapers and magazines and dozens of radio and television talk shows resound with differing points of view. The difficulty lies in deciding which opinion to agree with and which "experts" seem the most credible. The more inundated we become with differing opinions and claims, the more essential it is to hone critical reading and thinking skills to evaluate these ideas. Opposing Viewpoints books address this problem directly by presenting stimulating debates that can be used to enhance and teach these skills. The varied opinions contained in each book examine many different aspects of a single issue. While examining these conveniently edited opposing views, readers can develop critical thinking skills such as the ability to compare and contrast authors' credibility, facts, argumentation styles, use of persuasive techniques, and other stylistic tools. In short, the Opposing Viewpoints Series is an ideal way to attain the higher-level thinking and reading skills so essential in a culture of diverse and contradictory opinions.

In addition to providing a tool for critical thinking, Opposing Viewpoints books challenge readers to question their own strongly held opinions and assumptions. Most people form their opinions on the basis of upbringing, peer pressure, and personal, cultural, or professional bias. By reading carefully balanced opposing views, readers must directly confront new ideas as well as the opinions of those with whom they disagree. This is not to simplistically argue that everyone who reads opposing views will—or should—change his or her opinion. Instead, the series enhances readers' understanding of their own views by encouraging confrontation with opposing ideas. Careful examination of others' views can lead to the readers' understanding of the logical inconsistencies in their own opinions, perspective on why they hold an opinion, and the consideration of the possibility that their opinion requires further evaluation.

Evaluating Other Opinions

To ensure that this type of examination occurs, Opposing Viewpoints books present all types of opinions. Prominent spokespeople on different sides of each issue as well as well-known professionals from many disciplines challenge the reader. An additional goal of the series is to provide a forum for other, less known, or even unpopular viewpoints. The opinion of an ordinary person who has had to make the decision to cut off life support from a terminally ill relative, for example, may be just as valuable and provide just as much insight as a medical ethicist's professional opinion. The editors have two additional purposes in including these less known views. One, the editors encourage readers to respect others' opinions—even when not enhanced by professional credibility. It is only by reading or listening to and objectively evaluating others' ideas that one can determine whether they are worthy of consideration. Two, the inclusion of such viewpoints encourages the important critical thinking skill of objectively evaluating an author's credentials and bias. This evaluation will illuminate an author's reasons for taking a particular stance on an issue and will aid in readers' evaluation of the author's ideas.

It is our hope that these books will give readers a deeper understanding of the issues debated and an appreciation of the complexity of even seemingly simple issues when good and honest people disagree. This awareness is particularly important in a democratic society such as ours in which people enter into public debate to determine the common good. Those with whom one disagrees should not be regarded as enemies but rather as people whose views deserve careful examination and may shed light on one's own.

Thomas Jefferson once said that "difference of opinion leads to inquiry, and inquiry to truth." Jefferson, a broadly educated man, argued that "if a nation expects to be ignorant and free . . . it expects what never was and never will be." As individuals and as a nation, it is imperative that we consider the opinions of others and examine them with skill and discernment. The Opposing Viewpoints Series is intended to help readers achieve this goal.

David L. Bender and Bruno Leone,
Founders

Greenhaven Press anthologies primarily consist of previously published material taken from a variety of sources, including periodicals, books, scholarly journals, newspapers, government documents, and position papers from private and public organizations. These original sources are often edited for length and to ensure their accessibility for a young adult audience. The anthology editors also change the original titles of these works in order to clearly present the main thesis of each viewpoint and to explicitly indicate the opinion presented in the viewpoint. These alterations are made in consideration of both the reading and comprehension levels of a young adult audience. Every effort is made to ensure that Greenhaven Press accurately reflects the original intent of the authors included in this anthology.

Introduction

> *"About one in two consumers in [a 1999]* Prevention Magazine *study said that DTC [direct-to-consumer] ads . . . help them have better discussions with their doctors about their health."*
>
> —National Health Council

> *"Many DTC advertisements leave out important safety information and exaggerate the product's benefits, as witnessed by the frequency with which the FDA [Food and Drug Administration] has found fault with them."*
> —Joel Lexchin, physician, and Barbara Mintzes, university researcher

In the nineteenth century traveling salesmen hawked the latest elixirs to an eager audience. More than a century later, pharmaceutical companies have adopted a similar practice to target potential customers. With direct-to-consumer (DTC) advertising, prescription drugs are marketed via television, radio, and print advertisements. These commercials describe medicines for ailments such as arthritis, depression, and sexual dysfunction, urging viewers who suffer from these conditions to "ask their doctor" about the advertised medicine. In 2003 pharmaceutical manufacturers spent $3.43 billion on such advertisements. The rise of DTC marketing is an example of the many ways that advertising is changing, as drug advertisers skip the middlemen—doctors—in favor of direct communication with potential customers. This change in pharmaceutical advertising has generated intense debate. Advocates of DTC advertising contend that these commercials help improve the quality of health care and have strengthened the doctor-patient relationship. However, critics assert that the advertisements damage the doctor-patient bond and fail to inform patients of the risks associated with taking the medications being promoted. The controversy over direct-to-consumer advertising typifies the concern many people have about advertising, namely, whether commercials help people make informed purchasing decisions or if advertisers are more interested in increasing sales for their clients by any means necessary.

According to its supporters, DTC advertising helps people take control of their health care decisions. In its report *Direct-to-Consumer Prescription Drug Advertising: Overview and Recommendations*, the National Health Council asserts that DTC advertising informs consumers about the symptoms of various conditions and increases awareness about treatment options. According to the council, "Consumers find DTC advertising useful. . . . In [market researching firm] Scott-Levin's 2000 survey, 67% of consumers agreed that DTC advertising raises awareness of new treatment options, and 63% agreed that these ads alert patients that symptoms may be a sign of a more serious medical condition."

The American Advertising Federation also touts the benefits of these advertisements, pointing to a Food and Drug Administration (FDA) survey that found that viewing DTC commercials spurred 32 percent of patients to discuss the medicine with their doctors, and 27 percent of patients to talk to their doctors about a specific ailment for the first time. The federation asserts that these doctor-patient interactions increase the effectiveness of health care by enabling doctors to address their patients' medical conditions sooner than would otherwise have been the case.

DTC advertising's critics, however, charge that these advertisements damage the doctor-patient relationship and can result in serious health problems for those responding to the ads. For example, opponents of DTC marketing assert that consumers who are determined to obtain prescriptions to advertised drugs will often change doctors in order to find one willing to prescribe the medication. Doctors who do not wish to lose patients frequently yield to these requests. A survey published in *Prevention* magazine in 2000 found that 80 percent of patients who asked for a specific prescription received it. Not surprisingly, as Phyllis Maguire notes in an article for the *ACP-ASIM Observer*, doctors are increasingly frustrated by the changes DTC marketing has made to their relationships with patients. She writes, "When patients arrive with a specific medication in mind, doctors must first explain other, sometimes more effective, treatments. But when doctors try steering patients away from advertised treatments, they find that it's their credibility on the line, not the advertiser's."

Furthermore, note its critics, DTC advertising is misleading because it does not inform patients of all the risks and side effects associated with the medicines. The Food and Drug Administration permits drug companies to describe the benefits of their products without going into detail about side effects, other than major risks, as long as the advertisement mentions a Web site and toll-free phone number where consumers can receive more information. Consequently, consumers may believe a drug is appropriate for their needs when it could in actuality worsen their health. Joel Lexchin and Barbara Mintzes expressed this concern in an article in the fall 2002 issue of the *Journal of Public Policy & Marketing.* They observed that increased compliance with anti-arthritis treatments "is associated not with health benefits but with a higher risk of serious adverse effects." Lexchin and Mintzes turned out to be prescient—two years later, the popular anti-arthritis medicine Vioxx was pulled from the market when a clinical trial found that long-term use doubled a person's risk of strokes and heart attacks. Without DTC marketing, it is possible that fewer people would have been exposed to the drug's potential deadly effects.

Despite its positive impact on prescription drug sales, direct-to-consumer advertising still represents only 15 percent of the advertising expenses of American pharmaceutical companies. However, even with the problems besetting Vioxx and its manufacturer, DTC advertising—and the accompanying controversy—is likely to increase as new drugs are created. The debate over DTC marketing helps illuminate many of the issues surrounding advertising, such as whether American society is helped or hindered by commercialism. In *Opposing Viewpoints: Advertising,* the authors debate these and other related topics in the following chapters: Is Advertising Harmful? Does Advertising Exploit Children? Should Political Advertising Be Reformed? What Is the Future of Advertising? Because advertising is an inescapable element of American life, understanding its impact can have significant political, social, and economic implications.

CHAPTER 1

Is Advertising Harmful?

Chapter Preface

Most companies want their products to appeal to a wide audience. One way companies can broaden consumer interest in their products is by including a variety of people in their advertisements. Unfortunately, the depiction of certain populations is frequently stereotypical. For example, while the portrayal of gays and lesbians in commercials is improving, many companies rely on homophobic imagery to sell their goods.

These homophobic commercials rely primarily on two themes: homosexuals as unmanly sexual predators and prison rape as a source of humor. For example, the Internet company Yahoo ran a television ad in the United Kingdom that depicted a naked man tied to a tree after a wild bachelor party; he is being ogled by an effeminate man wearing a purple hat and scarf. The commercial was pulled following protests. Other corporations make light of nonconsensual homosexual encounters, in particular prison rape. Such imagery has been used in a commercial for Virgin Mobile. In that advertisement musician Wyclef Jean is shown showering in a prison; in a clear reference to prison rape, he is asked by another man to pick up a bar of soap from the shower floor. Michael Wilke, a columnist for Commercial Closet, an organization that studies the portrayals of gays and lesbians in advertisements, writes of these advertisements, "Homophobia is [these commercials'] source of humor and remains a popular root of jokes in countless ads."

While these companies have used offensive stereotypes and antigay jokes to sell their products, other businesses have turned to more positive portrayals of gays and lesbians. For example, *New York Times* writer Stuart Elliott has written about the growing use of homosexual celebrities in advertisements. Singer k.d. lang has been used in Audi ads, and singer Melissa Etheridge appears in ads for Cartier. Other advertisements do not employ celebrities but do portray gay relationships in a matter-of-fact or positive manner. A commercial for Christian Dior shows two women in a sensual embrace, and an advertisement for IKEA shows a male couple purchasing a dining room table. The companies who authorize these ads recognize the need, as stated by Wilke, "to be more thoughtful about stereotypes and use common sense along with focus group testing."

Advertising can benefit society by making people aware of valuable products and services. At the same time, commercials can reinforce stereotypes. In the following chapter the authors examine whether advertising is harmful. With advertisements an inescapable part of Americans' lives, their effects cannot be taken lightly.

"Advertising represents the triumph of the consumer over the power of producers and vested interests."

Advertising Benefits Consumers

John Hood

Advertising is beneficial to consumers because it saves them time and energy, John Hood argues in the following viewpoint. According to Hood, advertising provides consumers with valuable information about the price, quality, and availability of products, while also helping to lower the cost of those products. He further notes that despite the claims of many critics, advertising does not create artificial demand for certain items, although Hood does acknowledge that commercials can help shape desires. Hood is the president of the John Locke Foundation, a think tank based in North Carolina that supports individual rights and the free market, and an author whose books include *The Heroic Enterprise: Business and the Common Good.*

As you read, consider the following questions:
1. In what societies is commercial advertising found, according to Hood?
2. According to the author, what conclusions can be drawn between eyeglass advertising and prices?
3. In the author's view, when is the relationship between advertising and product quality the strongest?

John Hood, "In Praise of Advertising," *Consumers' Research Magazine*, April 1, 1998. Copyright © 1998 by *Consumers' Research Magazine*. Reproduced by permission.

For the last few years—until 1998, at least—the Super Bowl hasn't exactly featured the most interesting and competitive of football games. They've been blowouts, over by the first half at the latest. But one form of competition has remained as strong and vibrant as ever: the fight to put on the most memorable television advertisement. Over the years, many such ads have made their debut during the Super Bowl, including Apple's "1984" ads touting their new Macintosh, celebrity ads for Pepsi and Coke, and the croaking frogs of "Bud-wei-ser."

A Powerful Force

Isn't there something wrong with this picture? Should advertising overshadow that for which it is supposed to be merely a sponsor? Well, the answers to these questions lie far beyond the game of football. As James Twitchell, author of *Adcult USA: The Triumph of Advertising in American Culture* points out, it isn't just the Super Bowl ads that live on long after the game is forgotten. Advertising generates powerful and lasting social symbols. Think of Morris the cat, Mikey the Life cereal kid, the Marlboro Man, the Jolly Green Giant, the Energizer Bunny. Think of tunes like "I'd Like to Teach the World to Sing," "Plop, Plop, Fizz, Fizz," and "We've Only Just Begun" (a song the Carpenters made a hit after it had already been widely heard in a bank commercial). Think of slogans like "Have it your way," "Just do it," "Snap, crackle, pop," and "Be all you can be."

The ubiquity of advertising, as well as its apparent excess and wastefulness, has led many social critics and would-be consumer "advocates" to demonize it. "Advertising is the science of arresting the human intelligence long enough to get money from it," wrote one critic. Novelist George Orwell said advertising "is the rattling of a stick inside a swill bucket." Clare Boothe Luce wrote that advertising had "done more to cause the social unrest of the twentieth century than any other single factor." A common attack is that ads manufacture consumers' demand for products that they would otherwise not feel a need to buy. "Few people at the beginning of the nineteenth century needed an adman to tell them what they wanted," groused economist John Kenneth Galbraith.

"The institutions of modern advertising and salesmanship," he continued, ". . . cannot be reconciled with the notion of independently determined desires, for their central function is to create desires—to bring into being wants that previously did not exist."

Advertising Helps Consumers Make Decisions

But there is another side to advertising, one that these and other social commentators have largely overlooked. Advertising represents the triumph of the consumer over the power of producers and vested interests. Commercial advertising, at least, is found only in societies where individuals have the right to choose their own goods and services from competing suppliers. Ads convey critical information about price, quality, and availability. Furthermore, in many cases ads are indistinguishable from the product; to consume it is to express yourself through the symbols that ads have invoked (the thrill of driving a new car down a highway is a good example of this phenomenon).

In short, advertising is good for consumers. It's worth exploring how in greater detail.

Many of advertising's critics have portrayed it as playing either no role or a counterproductive role in advancing consumer interests. For example, some economists have long argued that ads create barriers to entry in particular industries, thus reducing competition and making prices higher. This happens, it is argued, because the ads differentiate an existing product—say, a breakfast cereal—from a possible competing product that might taste better or cost less, or both. Consumers might be better off trying this new product, but they are already made familiar with the existing product's name through ads and thus don't make the buying decision that would best satisfy their wants.

This model of consumer decision-making neglects to address an obvious dilemma that all of us face every day: limited time and attention span. Given the multitude of activities each of us carries out every day, it is a myth to suggest that we have the time, ability, or inclination to gather perfect information about every alternative available for every good or service we wish to purchase. Because of this practical constraint on market decisions, clever and memorable advertising serves a useful function if it establishes loyalty to a brand that offers us what we want. Of course, advertising alone won't create a lasting attachment. We have to experience the good, and actually enjoy it or find it beneficial and economical. Once having done so, however, brand loyalty then helps us remember and subsequently purchase that useful good again without having to spend a great deal of costly time and resources searching for it.

One study of brand loyalty did, indeed, find that for consumer products such as soft drinks, electric shavers, hair spray, detergents, and cigarettes, consumers do display a kind of brand loyalty called "inertia." That is, they tend to buy the same brand consistently. But as economists Robert B. Ekelund, Jr. and David S. Saurman wrote in their award-wining book *Advertising and the Market Process*, "to conclude that advertising of these brands cause the inertia would be similar to convicting a suspect with only the prosecutor's opening statement to the jury as evidence."

In fact, one obvious reason why some products that are bought often tend to display consumer inertia is that consumers are well-satisfied with them, and have made the rational judgment that alternative products are unlikely to provide significantly better value. More important, Ekelund and Saurman report that the intensity of advertising more often correlates with less consumer inertia rather than more. Expenditures are higher, in other words, where consumers exhibit less clear attachment to one brand. Another study found that, from 1948 to 1959, the market share of leading brands actually decreased in highly advertised industries; indeed, the market share of leading brands in toiletries and cosmetics, the highest-advertised industry in the study, decreased faster than in industries such as soap and food, where advertising expenditures were lower.

Advertising Encourages Competition

More generally, Ekelund and Saurman report that competition among firms is, if anything, more fierce—and market shares more uncertain—in industries with higher-than-average advertising expenditures. "The more intensively all firms in industries advertise," they write, "the less stable are market shares or the more these market shares tend to change." The reason is obvious. It's not just the market leaders who get to advertise. So do their rivals. For entrants into a new sector, advertising isn't a barrier but an opportunity. How else can a new producer get the attention of a busy consumer, and get him or her to try something new? Advertising, far from being a constraint on vigorous competition, is more likely a necessary prerequisite for it to occur.

Per Capita Advertising Expenditures in Selected Countries

Countries with Highest Spending	Per Capita (U.S.$)	Countries with Lowest Spending	Per Capita (U.S.$)
United States	534.8	Laos	0.9
Hong Kong	510.9	Pakistan	1.0
Puerto Rico	428.4	India	1.6
Switzerland	352.8	Vietnam	1.8
Norway	326.8	Cambodia	2.4
Japan	331.8	China	3.7
United Kingdom	270.6	Indonesia	4.9
Denmark	252.8	Philippines	6.5
Australia	235.8	Saudi Arabia	7.5
Singapore	222.0	Romania	7.9

Katherine Toland Frith and Barbara Mueller, *Advertising and Society*, 2003.

What about prices? Surely, one might surmise, the hundreds of billions of dollars a year spent on intensive advertising are passed along, at least in part, to consumers in the form of higher prices. But this view is completely contradicted by the facts. Take eyeglasses. For years, some states restricted or banned advertising for eye examinations and eyeglasses, while others did not. This gave researchers a good data set from which to draw conclusions about advertising and price. As it turns out, states that limited advertising had eyeglass prices that were 25% higher than their peers without ad restrictions. To take the most extreme examples, Washington, D.C., and Texas had no advertising restrictions at all, while North Carolina had the most wide-ranging restrictions in the nation. North Carolina eyeglass prices were double those in D.C. and Texas.

Another study looked at gasoline prices. After adjusting for income and other factors, American Enterprise Institute researchers Thom Kelly and Alex Maurizi found that regions where gas stations displayed their prices prominently to drivers had significantly lower average gas prices than regions where the prices, for whatever reason, weren't clearly visible from the road. Interestingly, this study not only demonstrated how advertising can reduce prices by encouraging competition, but did so with billboard advertising—one of the most loathed forms of commercial activity on the part of many critics.

Finally, the relationship between advertising and product quality deserves a mention. It appears to be strongest for products that are expensive and purchased infrequently. For disposable "experience goods" like soap or food that are purchased often, consumers develop their own body of information about quality. They either like a brand or they don't. But for high-cost, high-value "search goods" such as automobiles, farm equipment, computers, or household appliances, consumers seem to demand information on quality. One study of the Yellow Pages bore this out. Ads for search goods and services were four to 12 times more likely to include information about licensing or certification, consumer ratings, and other quality selling points than did ads for experience goods, which focused more on price and availability.

Seeking Enjoyment

Some critics of advertising grant that it plays an important role in the competitive process, but still criticize it for "creating" consumer demand where it would otherwise not exist. In particular, many point to advertising for products such as perfumes and soft drinks that rely rarely on price or specific quality information and more on images, music, celebrities, or symbolism. What practical benefit could this kind of advertising possibly provide? Isn't it just an expensive and wasteful form of brain candy?

Only if one adopts a limited, even soulless, view of markets.

After all, they don't exist simply to supply proteins, mildly stimulative liquid refreshments, tonal recreational amenities, or person-carrying devices. They give us sizzling steaks, a beer after work, a concert on Saturday night, and a fast car to get us there. As in other areas of our lives—such as family or faith—free enterprise is a means by which we seek meaning and enjoyment. The extent to which advertising contributes to that function is greater than is usually perceived.

Take sports merchandise. No matter how many Nike shorts or Air Jordans you wear, you are very unlikely to be as good at basketball as the athletes who advertise these wares. No matter how many banners, jackets, buttons, or flags you buy with your favorite team's logo on them, you will never actually be part of the team or directly share in its wins or losses. But that isn't the point. People seem to enjoy expressing their affinity, their affection for their heroes and teams by sporting their colors. It makes the game more meaningful to them.

Similarly, the fact that millions of Americans are buying four-wheel-drive sport-utility vehicles will not change the fact that most will never actually use them as some of the people in ads do—to haul things, for example, or to go four-wheeling through rugged mountain terrain. Even images of families with children heading home from soccer practice don't necessarily comport with the actual use of sport utilities by young singles. But something about those images resonates with the buyer. It might be a true aspiration to do those things, or just a sense that the purchase of such a vehicle might expand their possibilities. Whatever the source, it is obvious that in these cases the advertising becomes, in a way, part of the good being purchased. To some extent, the buyer of a new Mustang convertible is buying the feeling that ads for the convertible have expressed, a sense of freedom or adventure.

Advertising Shapes Desires

Some may view this side of advertising as a vice, but I see it as a virtue. It doesn't mean that advertising actually creates a demand for a product. It's not that powerful. The desire for goods and services to make our lives safer, cleaner, easier, and more enjoyable is already implanted deep within us. What advertising does is merely to bring that desire out into the open, and give it a distinct form. As James Twitchell observes, "the real work of Madison Avenue is not to manipulate the doltish public but to find out how people already live . . . not to make myth but to make your product part of an already existing code." He summarizes the concept neatly this way:

"Advertising is simply one of a number of attempts to load objects with meaning. It is not a mirror, a lamp, a magnifying glass, a distorted prism, a window, a trompe l'oeil, or a subliminal embedment as much as it is an ongoing conversation within a culture about the meanings of objects. It does not follow or lead so much as it interacts. Advertising is neither chicken nor egg. Let's split the difference, it's both. It is language not just about objects to be consumed but about the consumers of objects."

It is also a language that is spoken only in a society where individuals—not guilds, not bureaucracies, not all-powerful institutions—ultimately decide what goods and services will be produced and consumed. They do so by exercising their choice as consumers. Advertising helps them do that. It's no more complicated than that.

"Despite the dominance of commercialism in our culture, social scientists have barely begun to explore its nature and its consequences."

Advertising Has Too Great an Influence on Society

Center for the Study of Commercialism

Advertising is destructive to American culture, the Center for the Study of Commercialism maintains in the following viewpoint. According to the center, the dangerous effects of advertising include the perpetuation of stereotypes, higher product costs and taxes, an overemphasis on appearance, and an undermining of family values. The center asserts that these and other effects need to be explored more thoroughly by social scientists. The Center for the Study of Commercialism is an organization that uses research, public information campaigns, and legislative efforts to establish limits on commercialism.

As you read, consider the following questions:
1. How does commercialism contribute to environmental problems, according to the center?
2. In the view of the author, how is entertainment influenced by advertisements?
3. How is commercialism similar to industrial pollution, as argued by the center?

A re we immune to commercialism?
Each of us would like to believe that we're immune to the effects of advertising and commercialism. Maybe other people are affected by ads, but we ourselves are too smart, too savvy.

Yet are we really immune? A lot of evidence suggests that we are influenced. Think about the nationally-advertised products we buy, the style of our clothes, the kinds of food we eat, the attention we give to our appearance, and our encyclopedic knowledge of brand names. In these ways and others, our lives reflect the ads around us.

Over the years, the sophistication of marketing has increased a great deal. The messages that encourage us to buy are designed by creative, talented people. Modern scientific knowledge of human psychology and of how the brain processes visual information is used in developing ads. An array of technical equipment and resources is also used. Ads talk to our conscious, rational mind and to our subconscious fears and desires.

Of course, no one would advocate a ban on marketing. Ads provide information that can be helpful to us as consumers. Ads increase our understanding of the product choices available to us. And in an economy based on free enterprise, ads play a vital role for the business community. Ads are a valid part of modern life.

Some people are concerned about all the advertising we're exposed to. They feel that the constant message to buy influences us in ways that are not to our benefit. One concern is that the message to buy overshadows other messages about helping each other, caring for our environment, and contributing to community.

What follows is a summary of concerns about the influence of commercialism in our lives. The information is not presented as an objective argument on the pros and cons of commercialism. In fact, this list and essay were put together by an organization that works to fight commercialism. Do you think these concerns are valid? Why or why not?

The Troubling Effects of Advertising

Commercialism distorts our culture by turning every event into a reason to consume. Anthropologists say that holidays reflect a culture's values. In America, every holiday is a sales event.

Advertising projects false images. For example, some ads imply that you're not cool unless you drive an expensive car, that smoking means you're an independent spirit, or that to be mature means drinking alcohol.

Commercialism contributes to environmental problems by encouraging wasteful use of natural resources. Over-packaging, disposable goods, and buying things we don't really need all contribute to unnecessary use of limited resources. The manufacture and disposal of the things we buy cause other environmental problems, including habitat loss and increased air and water pollution. Billboards cause visual pollution.

Advertising perpetuates stereotypes. Examples include stereotypes related to race (African-Americans as musicians and athletes), gender (women as sex objects, men as business people), and class (middle-class whites as the social norm).

Advertisers influence the content of publications and broadcasts. Government censorship of the media is illegal. Yet it is well documented that newspapers and other media are censored by advertisers. For example, a beer producer may pressure a magazine in which it buys ad space not to print articles on the dangers of drinking.

Corporate sponsorship of civic, environmental, or other non-profit groups may influence those groups. For example, tobacco industry contributions may discourage an organization from joining anti-smoking campaigns.

Economic and Social Costs

Commercialism has influenced our political process. Many politicians try to attract votes with an image created by advertising and media coverage. In the past, candidates tried to attract votes by their stand on the issues.

The public's perception of a company's activities and priorities can be distorted by image advertising. For example, ads can portray major polluters as environmentally conscious companies that give to worthy causes.

Advertising costs us money. Businesses pass many of their advertising costs on to us. Also, the price of a product increases when ads successfully cultivate the idea that a certain product can give us status or a cool image.

Ads cost us more in taxes, too. Advertising is a fully tax-deductible business expense. Because of this, state and federal treasuries receive billions of dollars less in business taxes each year. Tax rates for citizens must make up for this, so individual taxpayers indirectly subsidize advertising.

Ads can be misleading. They emphasize the benefits of products and services and ignore the drawbacks.

Ads encourage a brand-name mentality, or buying on the basis of the maker rather than quality or price.

Advertising fosters dissatisfaction, envy, and insecurity. It can make us feel unattractive, uncool, and unhappy with what we do or don't have.

Our commercialized society places a strong emphasis on appearance, encouraging us to care about our own and others' appearances rather than about characters, talents, and personalities.

Constant exposure to ads may encourage materialism and selfishness. This may make people less inclined to help others. Statistics show that giving to charitable causes has decreased in recent years. Similarly, there has been a decline in public support for government programs to aid the least fortunate members of our society.

Loss of Privacy and Integrity

Corporate sponsorship may influence content and undermine the objectivity of exhibits at science and art museums. For example, is an exhibit sponsored by a company that makes insecticides likely to examine human/insect relationships in a fair and balanced way?

Ads take a lot of our time. The average person spends almost an hour a day reading, watching, or listening to ads through TV, radio, theaters, videotapes, newspapers, magazines, mail, or telephone. By the time the average American is seventy-five years old, advertising will have taken four years of his or her life.

Paid product placements influence the content of movies, TV shows, books, and board games. This compromises artistic integrity.

Advertising promotes alcohol and tobacco use, which kill half a million Americans annually. Problems related to alcohol hurt more people's lives and cost society more money than all illegal drugs combined.

Countering the Claims

Advertisers Say:

• advertising helps to sell more products, allowing companies to make many items at once, and to do so at a lower cost; it also lets people compare prices, and find the least expensive product; this competition keeps prices low

• advertising protects consumers by informing them—and because companies that spend a lot of money promoting their product work harder to keep their promises and ensure the product is worth buying

• advertising gives consumers many products to choose from and by encouraging people to buy, it keeps money circulating and people employed

• advertising promotes products that can improve people's lives; it encourages them to strive for a better life

Critics Say:

• the money spent on advertising makes products more expensive; consumers are ultimately the ones who pay for advertising through higher product prices

• advertising makes it easy for big companies (with lots of money to spend on promotion) to put small companies (which can't afford to advertise as much) out of business and limit competition

• by encouraging people to buy things they don't need, advertising contributes to waste, creating pollution and damaging our environment

• advertising tends to show only certain kinds of people and to define beauty in a narrow way; it encourages people to be dissatisfied with themselves, to feel insecure and vulnerable

Shari Graydon, *Made You Look*, 2003.

Marketers compile detailed electronic portraits of shoppers. Companies sell mailing lists for everything from foreign car ownership to sexual preference. These computer databases present a staggering potential for abuse.

Commercialism has spread into almost every aspect of life.

Being unable to escape it is annoying to many.

Advertising aimed at young children intrudes on the parent-child relationship, can undermine parental authority, and can create friction in the home.

Advertising Promotes Harmful Values

Commercialism may erode values—such as sharing, co-operation, and frugality—fostered by families, religious institutions, and schools.

Commercial foods and the ads for them tend to encourage unhealthy eating habits.

Commercialization of school materials and equipment may undermine objective, unbiased education.

Heavy promotion of shopping and buying distracts us from other activities such as reading, thinking, and playing. All the ads we're exposed to make it easy to forget how many different kinds of activities we enjoy.

Our commercialized culture encourages people to spend money that they don't really have. The number of Americans with financial problems has increased steadily in recent years.

Advertising implies that there's an easy solution to everything, from being healthy to having friends.

Many ads imply, even if they don't say outright, that happiness is something we can buy. When we act as though this is true, our personal horizons and ability to find fulfillment in life are limited.

Commercialism does not just promote specific products. It promotes consumption as a way of life.

The Effects of Commercialism

Commercialism has clear parallels with industrial pollution. Just as modest amounts of waste can be absorbed by the natural environment, so modest amounts of commercialism can be assimilated by our cultural environment. Large amounts, however, can totally overwhelm either environment, and such is the case today.

For decades we failed to recognize, let alone control, the harm caused by industrial practices. In some cases, such as air pollution from coal-burning furnaces, the problems were obvious but were either ignored or justified on the basis of short-term economic gain. In other cases, such as toxic chemicals that pollute the air and water, the dangers were not even recognized. So it is with commercialism: We excuse its obvious defects in the name of economic progress; we don't even try to identify more subtle effects.

Again as with pollution several decades ago, the consequences of excessive commercialism remain unexamined and unproven. Our understanding rests on a handful of often preliminary or inconclusive academic studies. The fact is that, despite the dominance of commercialism in our culture social scientists have barely begun to explore its nature and its consequences. Moreover, government regulatory programs are inadequate to contain commercialism. Agencies that focus on deceptive advertising have such small budgets—totalling only about one thousandth as much as what is spent on advertising—that only the most blatantly dishonest advertising can be stopped. Other forms of commercialism go completely unexamined.

What, then, is the impact on our society, when, as *Advertising Age* [a technical journal for people who work in the advertising industry] wrote, "mass-media advertising explodes out of a shotgun and sprays everyone in its path, kids included"? And beyond advertising, what are the effects of living in a culture where even schools, museums, sports and non-commercial broadcasters have been commercialized? Does commercialism turn engaged citizens into mere consumers?

"Stereotypes in advertising conform, for the most part, to cultural expectations of gender."

Advertisements Stereotype Women and Girls

Katherine Toland Frith and Barbara Mueller

In the following viewpoint Katherine Toland Frith and Barbara Mueller claim that advertisers frequently depict women and girls as passive and submissive. For example, the authors assert that while boys in toy commercials are shown playing actively with their toys, girls are portrayed as being quiet and gentle. Frith and Mueller also argue that women are sexualized in advertising. Frith is an associate professor in the School of Communication and Information at Nanyang Technological University in Singapore. Mueller is the coordinator of the Media Studies Program at San Diego State University.

As you read, consider the following questions:

1. How are colors used to stereotype girls in commercials, according to the authors?
2. In the view of Frith and Mueller, how do Americans define femininity?
3. What is the "engaging gaze," as defined by the authors?

The representation of women in advertising has been a concern since the rise of the feminist movement in the United States in the 1960s. A tremendous amount of research has been conducted over the years on images of women in ads, and a large number of national and international conferences on the topic have been held. Generally the criticisms of advertising fall into three areas: the stereotyping of women into passive and less powerful players in society, the portrayal of women as sexual objects in ads, and the cumulative effect of these portrayals on women's self-esteem. . . .

Gender Bias in Children's Commercials

The world of children's television is a gender-stratified world. Studies suggest that children's television is primarily a male world. These studies confirm that there are more male characters depicted than female. Even animated product representatives like Tony the Tiger are predominately male. Also, in children's commercials the male characters carry the action while female characters offer support. Marketers and advertisers support this gender bias by creating action-oriented products for boys (cars, guns, and action figures) and passive types of playthings for girls (dress-up dolls, kiddie cosmetics, and soft animals).

Advertisers further reinforce these stereotypes in the colors, settings, and behavior of each gender in the commercials. The male characters in boy-oriented commercials wear dark-colored clothing and are filmed against bright primary-colored backgrounds (dark green, blue, and gray). Commercials aimed at girls use pastel colors such as pink or white. Girls wear lighter-colored clothing. Boys are often filmed outside while commercials aimed at girls are filmed in bedroom-style sets or in playrooms.

In TV commercials boys run, shout, ride bikes, compete with each other, and take risks. Commercials aimed at boys have frequent cuts and many close-ups. In commercials aimed at girls the camera techniques create a soft, warm, fuzzy feeling. Girls play quietly in their pastel bedrooms or watch boys in more active play.

When boys are shown playing with their toys they are generally aggressive, even violent—crashing cars, or aggressively competing with action figures. Girls, on the other hand, are shown playing quietly and gently. For girls a toy is a playmate: for boys a toy is a plaything.

Cultivation theory suggests that repeated exposure to media messages leads a person to hold opinions or views of society that can be discordant with reality. When children internalize advertising and media stereotypes, gender myths can be perpetuated and children from a very early age may limit the roles they see themselves playing in society. Even very young girls are shown in advertisements for branded fashion goods, perhaps suggesting to children that fashion and beauty are what are most valued for women in society.

Unattainable Beauty

As girls grow into their teens, the media continue to play a significant role in the development of identity. In fact, much research has been done on images in the media and self-image in adolescents. One concern of critics is that advertisements present young girls with unrealistic beauty norms. Most advertisements that appear in magazines have been extensively retouched to remove even the slightest flaw. Techniques such as retouching led [Robin] Lakoff and [Raquel] Scherr to accuse advertisers of creating a "cult of unrealizable beauty." Critics contend that the uniformly thin, perfectly proportioned models contribute to unhappiness with their own bodies among young girls and thus undermine self-confidence and reinforce problems like eating disorders. In addition, [Kim] Walsh-Childers notes that advertising/photographers often focus on women's breasts, regardless of the product category. She contends that the idea that sexy equals big breasts has created feelings of inferiority in young girls, so that "plastic surgeons report that they now see girls as young as 14 seeking surgery to enlarge their breasts." Marsha Richins studied attitudes and behaviors of college students exposed to advertisements and found that after viewing beautiful models, subjects rated average women as less attractive. In other words, images of highly attractive individuals can cause viewers to rate the attractiveness of more ordinary others lower than they would otherwise. In addition, she found that exposure to highly attractive images negatively affected the subject's feelings about their own self-appearance. As the author notes, "while one may argue that temporary dissatisfaction is beneficial if it stimulates consumers to buy products that improve their appearance . . . it is difficult to argue that such is the case here." She points out that the repeated exposure to idealized images may have a cumulative effect on self-feelings.

Changes and Stagnation

[One study] found changes in portrayals in prime-time commercials in the 1990s. They report similar numbers of men and women in speaking roles, a decrease in the percentage of male voice-overs to 70%, and more atypical than stereotypical roles for women. Stereotypical roles are defined as those of homemaker, nurse, secretary, and victim or when a man is present and the woman is not in charge or when the woman is presented as a nag or scatterbrain.

On the other hand, a 1997 study of advertising during children's Saturday-morning programming indicates few changes from the 1970s. . . . 71% of the active roles went to males and 84% of the voice-overs were male. Females were depicted as inactive twice as often as were males. Only 13 of the 100 commercials contained an all-girl cast and of those 13, only 3 depicted a girl as physically active.

Kate Peirce, *Sex Roles*, December 2001.

In fact, research on child development has shown that self-perceptions of physical attractiveness are markedly different for male and female adolescents: Many researchers have noted that self-perceptions of physical attractiveness appear to decline systematically over time in girls but not boys. Boys tend to view their bodies as "process" and have a stronger view of themselves as holistic, while adolescent girls pay attention to individual body parts. Advertisers contribute to this "body-as-object" focus for female adolescents by using difficult-to-attain standards of physical attractiveness in ads. An analysis of *Seventeen*, a magazine aimed at adolescent females, found that over a 20-year period from 1970 to 1990, . . . models had become significantly thinner. While the actual emotional effects of repeated exposure to ultrathin models in magazine ads has been somewhat inconsistent, [Mary] Martin and [James W.] Gentry found that female college students who were repeatedly exposed to very thin models in ads felt increased guilt, shame, insecurity, and body dissatisfaction.

Gender stereotypes are learned through constant reinforcement. Although the terms *gender* and *sex* are often used interchangeably, these two concepts have very different meanings. Sex is biologically determined (male and female) while gender is culturally determined (masculine and feminine). Each culture has a set of general beliefs about what constitutes masculinity and femininity: these are known as gender roles. Stereotypes in advertising conform for the most part, to cultural expectations of gender. To be feminine in the United States is to be attractive, deferential, nonaggressive, emotional, nurturing, and concerned with people and relationships. To be masculine is to be strong, ambitious, successful, rational, and emotionally controlled. This cultural script has been written into the culture long before a baby is born. It is transmitted to children through family, peers, teachers, and the media. Advertising mirrors society, and therefore ads that use stereotypes not only reflect but also tend to reinforce the stereotypical representations that are already present in a culture. In the case of women [according to Linda Lazier and Alice G. Kendrick], "there is overwhelming evidence that advertisements present traditional, limited and often demeaning stereotypes of women. . . ." Since the majority of advertising research on gender stereotypes has been conducted in the United States, we will outline the general concerns about negative representation of women in North America. . . .

Advertisements Sexualize Women

One of the main criticisms of advertising that emerged in the late 1960s with the advent of the women's movement was feminists' concern that women's bodies were being used to sell everything from air conditioners to wrenches. While women in bikinis have been draped over cars and washing machines for decades, it was only in the 1970s that women began to take issue with this representation. Feminists complained that this type of portrayal "objectified" women.

Advertisers were also criticized for using language that put women down. The Virginia Slims slogan, "You've Come a Long Way, Baby," was critiqued for infantalizing women. Other critics pointed out that certain types of language and certain depictions of women had subtly violent undertones. Carol Adams suggested that in patriarchal cultures like that of the U.S.A., a hierarchy exists in which men are at the highest level and women and animals are positioned as inferior. She suggested that this relationship between women and animals had been naturalized by the use of terms like "bunnies, bitches, nags, beavers, chicks, pussycats, foxy ladies, and old bats" for women. In fashion advertising, women are often shown lying on bearskin rugs, wearing furs and feathers, or dressed in tight-fitting leather clothes. These kinds of ads have been criticized for positioning women as "prey."

In addition, women's bodies are often dismembered in ads and shown as "body parts," and this type of representation has also been criticized as objectifying women and contributing to the underlying culture of violence toward women.

Suggestive Poses

Another feminist critique that emerged in the early 1970s centered primarily on the limited roles in which advertisers showed women, i.e., mothers and housewives. Over time the range of roles women play in ads has expanded, but even today women are seldom shown playing powerful roles in society. For example, women's voices are seldom used as announcers in TV commercials because advertisers believe that women's voices lack authority, and women are still the ones shown in ads doing household jobs like laundry, child care, and so forth, and if men are shown engaging in these activities they are often positioned as "henpecked" or the objects of humor.

Women are also posed in submissive ways. Vickie Shields notes that historically the predominant "gaze" has been the male gaze. The "old masters" were just that, male painters. The male painted (active) whereas the women posed (passive). The female models were the objects of the male gaze. Shields argues that "ways of seeing" are gendered and that the male gaze is aggressive while the female gaze is submissive. Today, the painter has been replaced with the photographer. When women pose for the camera they often assume or are asked to assume a submissive or passive stance. While some might say that this "lowered eyes, head down" type of positioning is feminine, Shields would argue that it is submissive. In ads, women often gaze downward or away from the camera while men tend to gaze directly into the camera.

Erving Goffman conducted the earliest research on the positioning of women in submissive or inferior poses in ads. He identified symbolic behaviors in advertising presentation that are still used today by advertising researchers. These include:

• *Body cant or bashful knee bend.* These are fashion poses in which the model bends, and curves her body, bends her knee and points her toes, cocks her head and generally assumes a contorted posture in which movement is arrested and she is presented as a "sight" to be gazed upon.

• *Recumbent figure.* A model is shown reclining or semireclining on the floor or on the ground or lounging on a bed or sofa. While the passivity of such portrayals is apparent, the sexual innuendo also is obvious.

• *Psychological or licensed withdrawal.* This refers to poses for women where they appear to be drifting off (gazing away from the camera), daydreaming, or staring blankly out of the frame. Goffman suggested that this type of pose made women look as though they were mentally incompetent or vacant. The woman is shown to be "withdrawn" from reality and inactive (not acting on her surroundings).

• *The engaging gaze.* This is a passive pose where the model makes eye contact with the camera, engaging the viewer with seductive eye contact or a sexually seductive look.

• *Touching self.* In these poses the model touches her face or covers part of her face with her hands. Goffman suggested that this pose made women look girlish, shy, and submissive.

It is interesting to note that these poses are still commonly used 20 years after Goffman identified them.

"Does reversing sexual stereotypes accomplish anything?"

Advertisements Stereotype Men

Ivy McClure Stewart and Kate Kennedy

Advertising companies all too frequently portray men as incompetent slobs, Ivy McClure Stewart and Kate Kennedy charge in the following viewpoint. According to Stewart and Kennedy, commercials for foods, clothes, and credit cards often portray men as unable to feed, clean, or dress themselves. The authors argue that feminists and the advertising industry ought to recognize that these reverse stereotypes are offensive. Stewart is the managing editor of *Women's Quarterly*, and Kennedy is the campus project manager for the Independent Women's Forum.

As you read, consider the following questions:
1. How is the man portrayed in the VISA commercial described by the authors?
2. Why does Mike Flynn believe that advertisements featuring unappealing stereotypes are not successful?
3. In the opinion of Stewart and Kennedy, what will make "dumb dude" advertising persist?

Ivy McClure Stewart and Kate Kennedy, "Madison Avenue Man: He's Dumb, He's a Slob, He's Selling Kleenex," *Women's Quarterly*, Spring 2001, pp. 17–18. Copyright © 2001 by the Independent Women's Forum, www.iwf.org. Reproduced by permission.

Moaning from beneath his fuzzy flannel sheets, the big lug whines that every breath hurts and blubbers that his nose is raw from the constant rubbing. In comes Super Mom, armed with the latest in tissue technology: Kleenex Cold-Care. He's relieved. Then the voice-over: "The bigger the man, the bigger the baby."

"It is now absolutely acceptable to show men as thick, as incompetent, as sex-objects, as figures of fun, because it has become politically correct to do so. Men are fair game. But God forbid that you do that to women," Richard Block, global planning director of J. Walter Thompson, an international advertising firm whose clients include Kraft [Foods] and Ford Motor Company, told the *Sunday Business Journal*.

If you don't believe this, just ask the advertising execs who use ludicrous images of men to sell everything from Levi's to VISA cards. Fire up the remotes, guys—you're going to want to change the channel.

Men as Dumb Slobs

Take for example, the Campbell's soup commercial that paints the picture of a cozy family supper. "M'm! m'm! good!" cry the kids, who thank mom profusely for making such a mouth-watering meal. The soothing background voice spells it out: It's a delicious and oh-so-easy meal that comes from a can. Step one: Brown some chicken. Step two: Empty a can of Campbell's cream of mushroom soup into a pot and *voilà*, your kids will love it. Only, guess what? Mom didn't make this meal; it seems this task was easy enough even for dumb, old dad to handle.

"Dumb dads" seem to play especially prominent roles in today's commercials. And, rendering these poor chaps even more helpless, they are usually borderline obese. A case in point: A pudgy dad, face smudged with tell-tale signs that he's been sneaking slabs of the Honeybaked Ham he's fetched, wails to his attractive, well-turned out wife, "You don't think *I* ate it, do you?"

"There is definitely a poor image out there of men," says Tracie Snitker, government relations director for the Men's Health Network, an organization that monitors the depiction of men in mass media. "These kinds of campaigns are subtle, but they do pervade our inner consciousness."

VISA, perhaps the worst offender, showed a seriously anti-male ad during [the 2001] Super Bowl. Again, this one features a corpulent guy's guy lounging on his sofa in his dirty undershirt, which barely covers his beer gut. The camera pans down, exposing his socked feet in a perpetual twitch. He's picking popcorn out of his teeth, and is engrossed in a black-and-white television cartoon. All the while, his dutiful, beautiful wife is giving her new vacuum a test-run. As if this poor slob couldn't be any worse, he barks, "You missed a spot!" Unfazed, his wife turns the nozzle on him and sucks him up. "Huh, it really does work," she says looking down into the tube that swallowed her husband whole.

VISA spent approximately $2.3 million just to air this thirty-second spot during the Super Bowl, begging the question: How does this sell VISA cards? What is evident is that their message about the state of the American male was delivered loud and clear, and perhaps to the audience it was designed to entice—women. They obviously had the attention of ABC's Cokie Roberts, who highlighted what is becoming a new Super Bowl tradition for some women: watching solely for the commercials. "For some of us the most fun part of the Super Bowl is the ads. And this year there seems to be a theme, a tease. It does have to be funny, and it also has to be very creative and as I say, for some of us, particularly those of us in skirts, it's the best part of the game," she noted on [the TV news program] *This Week*.

Depictions of Incompetency

You might think a rugged product like Levi's would hesitate to make fun of guys. But consider this ad: It begins with sirens blaring as the ambulance roars to the scene. A paramedic rushes to the aid of a sickly man on the verge of death, curled up in the fetal position on his bed. Carrying a cooler containing what seems to be some vital organ, the paramedic summons the man's attention and reveals the lifesaver. It's a pair of Levi's jeans. It seems that this poor schlepp can't even get out of bed, never mind dressed. But once he musters the strength to pull on his hand-delivered Levi's, he is infused with life.

Along the same lines, there is an ad that features an incompetent buffoon who can't get his car stereo to work. Meanwhile, his frustrated and infinitely smarter wife looks on with pity. Luckily, she is clever enough to use the Yellow Pages to call a real professional.

Poor Examples of Husbands and Fathers

I do worry, however, about the kind of father role model advertisers are sculpting for our children. Will kids get the not-so-subtle idea that fathers are supposed to be knuckleheads, incapable of absorbing instructions without continual reinforcement? And will daughters treat their husbands this way? And, more importantly, will sons be conditioned not to pay much attention to their wives because they know through years of observation that there will be lots of opportunity to absorb the message?

Rance Crain, *Advertising Age*, March 26, 2001.

"Women like thinking they have the upper hand and we were taught that we've never had that. That is why these ads are so effective," says Snitker.

Not surprisingly some self-proclaimed media watchdog groups don't agree that Madison Avenue execs are laughing all the way to the bank at the expense of males. The National Organization for Women (NOW) maintains that it's the other way around, fretting that "80 percent of fourth-grade girls are dieting to reach ridiculous beauty standards set by advertisers and the media." (In that case, how long will it be before the men of this country seek counseling?)

Politically Correct Sexism

To counter what it regards as Madison Avenue's unfair portrayals of women, NOW hosts its annual "Love Your Body Day" in September in a concerted effort to "spark dialogue across this nation on the impact of harmful media messages and images of women."

NOW's press release about their day of bodily celebration declares, "It is a day of action to speak out against ads and images of women that are offensive, harmful, dangerous, and disrespectful. We hope that you will join us in raising our voices in opposition to beauty standards that are unrealistic and unhealthy, and in breaking down the stereotypes that discriminate against people based on size and appearance."

Excuse me, Ms. Ireland [NOW's president], have you watched TV lately?

Mike Flynn, senior vice president of [the advertising agency] D'Arcy Marius Benton & Bowles and a lecturer in universities on advertising, says that ads that feature unattractive stereotypes of either men or women "are not likely to be successful" since they do not depict "reality or aspirations." "In advertising," Flynn adds, "you have got to show people in one of two ways, either as they are now, or how they wish to be. It is politically incorrect to make fun of women. But men are an open target."

Possible Responses

But is a backlash brewing? An ad was yanked from Canadian television after viewers complained that it crossed the line. In it, a hunky man in a T-shirt was chained to a kitchen stove, while his glamorous mate left for her high-paying corporate job. The T. Eaton department store approved the ad as part of a series intended to tell consumers that it had radically changed its image, but yanked the "Chained" ad after objections were raised that it exploited and objectified men.

For years, the advertising industry was castigated for portraying women as half-wits, more concerned with vacuum cleaner bags and casseroles than matters of the mind. But, does reversing sexual stereotypes accomplish anything? Who wins when one group is pilloried in order to please another?

Flynn, whose firm creates ads for Coca-Cola and TWA, believes man-mocking ads are not likely to garner "much vocal opposition from men" in the United States. Instead, "men will react with their pocketbooks," withholding their dollars instead of spending them.

We're not sure, but you can bet that most dads will think twice (if they haven't already) before buying Campbell's, VISA, Levi's, or Kleenex. Still, according to Flynn, women do most of the household shopping. In the ad industry selling is the name of the game: If absurd male characters make merchandise fly off the shelves, the "dumb dude" is likely to remain a staple of television advertising and, perhaps more important, our inner consciousness.

"*Many advertisers have found innovative
and intelligent ways to market products
with positive, healthy images of race.*"

Depictions of Minorities in Advertisements Are Becoming More Positive

Children Now

In the following viewpoint Children Now asserts that while some companies continue to rely on racial stereotypes in their advertisements, more commercials are featuring positive images of minorities. One stereotypical advertisement the organization describes shows minority children as passive and lazy. Other commercials, however, reflect modern America's multicultural society and portray minorities as valuable members of society, Children Now asserts. Children Now is an organization that seeks to improve life for children and their families, in part by ensuring that they are exposed to positive media.

As you read, consider the following questions:

1. How much money do African Americans spend each year, according to Children Now?
2. According to the author, what are some of the stereotypes of African Americans that have persisted in commercials?
3. In the view of Children Now, what is a common mistake of advertisers?

Children Now, *Children, Race & Advertising*, Winter 1999. Copyright © 1999 by Children Now. Reproduced by permission.

The advertising industry spends billions of dollars annually to sell products, images, and lifestyles to an eager audience, many of whom are children. With engaging visuals, catchy slogans, attractive merchandise, and popular celebrities, it's no wonder that kids are enthusiastic consumers of both the products and the messages that ads provide. Everyday, children can find hundreds of advertisements on billboards and bus stops, in magazines and newspapers, on the radio, television, and the Internet. Clearly, advertising has an enormous amount of power to shape kids' attitudes, beliefs, and values. This special influence makes it important to explore how advertisers present race and class.

How do these images affect children's thinking about other people? About themselves? Consider that children who watch the multiracial interactions of *Sesame Street* or the international kids in *Big Blue Marble* show more positive attitudes toward people of color and other cultures. On the other hand, kids who watch shows that routinely stereotype people of color have less favorable attitudes toward those who may be different. Advertising has the same ability as television programming to impact children's perceptions. Commercials appear with great repetition, telling us what products will improve our lives and to what we can aspire. By offering roles for kids to admire or reject, advertising can tell children who is important and what they can become. When these pictures involve race and ethnicity, there are important considerations—what do the ads say about being a person of color? What do kids learn from the ads?

Over the past two decades, many advertising firms and in-house marketers have developed positive, successful ways to address diversity with openness and respect. In this [viewpoint] *Media Now* presents advertising practices that skillfully address the images of race and class children glean from commercial content.

Changes in Society and Advertising

During the 1980s and 1990s, motivated by economic and demographic trends and by growing consciousness, many advertising agencies began a significant shift toward culturally inclusive marketing. Consider the following facts:

Demographics

While the non-minority White population growth will steadily decline over the next 50 years, other groups will increase exponentially.

Economics

The current [1999] spending power of people of color ranks in the billions of dollars and is expected to increase exponentially as well. Currently, Hispanics spend $348 billion annually (projected to reach $477 billion by 2000), African Americans spend $469 billion, Asian & Pacific Islanders spend $110 billion.

With the realities of an increasingly multicultural society just around the corner, advertisers are now scrambling to stay one step ahead of the competition by incorporating smart, perceptive approaches. A diverse community requires marketers to recognize the power of different groups and the cutting-edge methods of rivals.

Today's advertising landscape includes facts such as:

• General Motors' budget for Hispanic media advertising in 1998 was $15 million, triple its 1996 amount.

• The Asian-American market is an ideal audience because of its leveraged education and buying power and tremendous brand loyalty.

• 1996 African-American consumer advertising figures were over $865 million.

• National advertising expenditures for Hispanic markets reached $1.4 billion in 1997.

Both advertising agencies and in-house marketing departments are rapidly increasing their resources for ethnic audiences. Accompanying these massive dollar expenditures is the need to maximize the return: How do we create the best advertising with and for people of color?

Common Depictions of Minorities

To explore advertising and people of color, we start by looking at how the majority and minorities have been shown.

Majority Images

"Television makes White people look smarter because they have a lot of money and you see more White people in the private schools."

Children Now found that kids of all races thought that

White characters were usually shown positively [e.g., wealthy, smart, leaders], while minorities were usually portrayed negatively [e.g., lawbreaking, lazy, poor]. In 1990, Professor Ellen Seiter of UC [University of California] San Diego noted that children's commercials often cast White kids as the leaders and go-getters, while minority children play passive or ignorant roles. The relationship between these different images has serious consequences for how White and minority children perceive their futures and each other.

Popular African American Endorsers

(1) TIGER WOODS

Having taken endorsement deal negotiations into the next stratosphere, he has re-energized the sport of golf and the sale of its products at the same time. He speaks for Nike, Titleist, Buick, American Express, and Rolex among others. It is estimated that he averages $54 million in endorsements a year.

(2) VENUS WILLIAMS

Women receive marginal recognition in sports as endorsers. This tennis dynamo has achieved two firsts: receiving a $40 million contract from Reebok, the largest amount ever paid to a female athlete; and leading the "Let's Talk" campaign with sister Serena as the first celebrity spokespeople for Avon.

(3) MICHAEL JORDAN

He's granddaddy of the endorsement deals. Name the category. Jordan's endorsed everything from sporting goods to men's cologne—successfully and without overexposure or blurring brands. A savvy businessman as well as champion ballplayer, he still has marketing appeal and averages $40 million a year.

Sonia Alleyne, *Black Enterprise*, September 2002.

Absence

"You want to think 'I could do that. I could be there. That could be me in five or six years.' But when you don't see anything of yourself. . . ."

All kids agreed that it is important to see people of their own race on TV. "It tells children that people of their race are important," and that "we can succeed and do our best." Today, while the number of African Americans in advertising has increased, there is still a dearth of Latinos, Asian & Pacific Islanders, and Native Americans in mainstream commercials or print ads. Absence remains a continuing concern.

Tokenism

"I don't think that they should have an Asian person just standing there. . . ."

There is more to creating positive images of people of color than putting them in the picture. In her 1990 study, Professor Seiter concluded that children of color in integrated ads were always outnumbered by Whites, usually silent, mainly in group shots, and often smiling broadly. Clearly, there is more to diversity than numbers.

Stereotypes

The exotic, shirtless African-American man as magical Honeycomb crunch genie. An aged, American Indian chief mysteriously vanishing and echoing, "Leave the land as you found it. . . ."

In the past, people of color have appeared as "lively Latins . . . Mexican bandits, pigtailed Chinese, and subservient Blacks" [according to M. Westerman]. Over time, advertisers responded to growing minority power by modifying some of these images. Aunt Jemima and Uncle Ben changed from African-American servants to flat, generic logos. Frito-Lay dropped the Frito Bandito character after hearing complaints from Hispanic groups.

Nonetheless, many stereotypes still remain. Today, we still see spicy Latinas and Asian computer geeks. We see that African-American boys play ball, African-American girls dance, and all African-American kids rap. Often, these "are the only arenas for achievement and ambition allowed Black children" [according to Seiter]. What will kids think when toys that encourage creativity, learning, and thinking are routinely associated with White children, while rap, sports, and goofing off are regularly associated with African-American or Latino kids?

Positive Images of Race

Recently, many advertisers have found innovative and intelligent ways to market products with positive, healthy images of race. For example, youth-oriented campaigns for personal care items such as Clearasil and Clean & Clear reflect the reality of today's multicultural society. And Bank of America defines "home" with families of color. These are just a few examples of advertising that is smart, creative, and successful.

Successful advertising agencies and in-house teams can design campaigns that are smart, appealing, respectful, and positive. Drawing from the best of multiculturalism, targeted advertising, and positive realism, as well as the real-life experiences of advertisers, the following questions may help you take advantage of advertising's power to create healthy images of race and class:

• *True Multiculturalism:* Does our advertising include people of color as full, rich, important characters?

• *Escaping Clichés:* Do the people of color in our ads avoid stereotypes?

• *Being Positive and Real:* Can our ads feature people of color and highlight the different, valuable lifestyles of different communities?

• *Spreading Positive Reality:* Could we incorporate our positive realist ads into mainstream channels (rather than only in ethnic outlets)?

• *Doing Homework:* Have we considered talking to ethnic specialists, minority advertising agencies, consultants, or focus groups to learn about diverse community preferences and to avoid cultural mistakes?

• *Avoiding Easy Mistakes:* Does this ad avoid the common mistake of ignoring cultural and ethnic nuances—i.e., simply substituting actors of color into a commercial aimed at mainstream White audiences? Or simply dubbing the sound or copy of mainstream commercials with a different language?

• *Joining the Community:* Can we design campaigns that celebrate the leaders, heroes, and events of minority communities? Could our marketing show commitments to the community's success through cause-related marketing?

| "[Sexual] images and portrayals are an area of concern because they serve as role models for young people."

Advertisements Rely on Distorted Depictions of Sexuality

Tom Reichert

In the following viewpoint Tom Reichert argues that numerous companies use sexual innuendo and provocative poses in their print and television campaigns. He notes that these advertisements have a strong effect on high school– and college-age men and women. Unfortunately, Reichert asserts, such commercials foster gender stereotypes and sexism and incorrectly teach young adults that people should be valued solely for their sexual appeal. Reichert is a professor of advertising at the University of Alabama at Tuscaloosa.

As you read, consider the following questions:
1. What types of companies are most likely to use sexual themes in their advertising, in the view of the author?
2. According to Reichert, how do sexually provocative advertisements provide a model for behavior for young people?
3. How does Reichert believe sexual images stereotype women?

Tom Reichert, "Sexy Ads Target Young Adults," *USA Today Magazine*, vol. 129, May 2001, p. 50. Copyright © 2001 by the Society for the Advancement of Education. Reproduced by permission.

By the time a youngster turns 14, he or she has been exposed to more than 350,000 television commercials. The average viewer watches at least six hours of commercial television messages a week. These estimates of media exposure do not include the countless print ads and promotional messages seen in other places. In all likelihood, sexy ads can be viewed by children watching programming during prime time or simply leafing through their brother's or sister's magazines.

What did the young adults involved in this study find sexy about the ads they identified? A 20-year-old male, describing [a] Candie's ad, said what he found sexy was "a partially naked Alyssa Milano [who is] surrounded by condoms and has her skirt hiked way up." Ads for Clairol Herbal Essences shampoo featuring women making orgasmic sounds prompted another 20-year-old male to say, "If I didn't see the TV, I might have thought it was a porno."

An 18-year-old female described a more recent Herbal Essences ad by saying, "The three men in black make the ad sexy. They are attractive and muscular, and the camera sometimes focuses on their hands touching the woman's body. It makes me, as the consumer, want to open the bottle of shampoo and have three strong, handsome men wash me."

The ad she was describing features a woman in a courtroom being attended to by three men. At the end of the commercial, celebrity sex therapist Dr. Ruth Westheimer makes a reference to a full-body wash. This ad, which has run on many networks, including MTV, is part of a long-running campaign that has featured women making orgasmic sounds while washing their hair in out-of-the-ordinary places, such as an airplane lavatory and a service station restroom. The tag line of the campaign is a true play on words —"A totally organic experience."

In 1995, CBS refused to let a Victoria's Secret commercial air during early prime time. The ad featured model Claudia Schiffer dancing "seductively" in her underwear. In 2000, the Schiffer commercial seems mild when compared to the ads mentioned by the respondents.

Most young adults rated what the models were (or were not) wearing and their physiques as top reasons they found ads to be sexy. Others included the models' demeanor or behavior, sexual behavior between models, and some aspect of each ad's production value (for example, commercials filmed in black white). Frequently, all of these elements are used by advertisers to create a sexy spot.

Sex Sells

In all fairness, sexy ads aren't prevalent for all brands and services. The technique typically is used to market mainstream brands associated with social interaction and attractiveness, such as clothing, health and beauty aids, fragrances, and alcohol. Recently, however, sexual themes have been used to sell coffee, tea, computers, watches, cigarette lighters, and lollipops. If you peruse magazines read by teenagers, you will see that sex is used for a wide range of products.

Why do advertisers use sex when advertising to young adults? One answer is novelty. Remember your first kiss? Chances are you do. For young people just discovering romance and crushes, venturing into the realm of sexuality is new and exciting, as well as laden with anxiety and danger if their parents should ever find out what they're up to.

Research in psychology has shown that novel, emotion-evoking stimuli attract a person's attention. It has the same effect for advertising. Provocative images and words are more likely to be noticed by a potential consumer. Subsequently, the attention directed toward the ad may enhance the probability the ad's message is processed. Given the saturation and proliferation of commercial messages and ads in the media market, any edge an advertiser can use to grab consumers' attention in the battle for their dollars is considered. The influx of hormones caused by adolescence amplifies the effect.

Another reason sexy ads are effective is that young people are more susceptible to advertising's promises. Young boys are more apt to believe a particular cologne really does attract women and that a certain brand of athletic shoe just may make them irresistible.

Consider ads mentioned by several young people involved in the study. They identified ads in a recent campaign for Lucky brand cologne that are notable for their unmistakable use of sexual entendre. One magazine ad features an interaction between a young couple. The man is ogling the woman's breasts. He's looking at her; she's looking at the viewer; and the tagline reads, "Get Lucky." The implication is that, if you wear Lucky, you just might "get lucky." Whether people refuse to accept such a premise or not, it's true that advertising appeals are more believable to the uninitiated.

In an attempt to sell Chupa Chups lollipops, an advertising agency in Texas developed a campaign titled "Oral Pleasure." The thrust of the campaign was to emphasize the fun of having a sucker in your mouth.

The culmination of this campaign was a commercial titled "Here Kitty, Kitty." The ad featured a woman seductively licking a lollipop, much to the delight of male actors who were obviously aroused by her actions. The campaign and this commercial were targeted at the 14–24 age group. To reach the target, ads were scheduled to run on "The Simpsons," "Friends," and "South Park," programs that also are popular with young people under the age of 14.

Provocative Role Models

Sexy ads are important to consider because they can influence young people in several ways. For one, they provide a highly salient behavioral model for young people. Most of these ads indicate, "If you do this or say this, you'll be more sexually attractive." That is a powerful promise for those experiencing sexual feelings for the first time. This effect is compounded when viewers are able to identify with the models in the commercials. Because humans constantly compare themselves to those around them and to those in the media, advertisers want to cast people similar in some respects to the target audience. Frequently, the point of comparison is age. All things being equal, young people are more apt to identify and subsequently compare themselves to those who are similar in age.

The use of young models in sexually provocative advertising is not new. In 1980, 15-year-old starlet/model Brooke Shields was cast in several provocative Calvin Klein jeans ads. In one commercial that was particularly memorable, albeit controversial, Shields uttered the now-famous line, "Do you want to know what comes between me and my Calvins? Nothing." The impact of the double entendre was enhanced by the way in which the camera slowly panned across her body. The ad created a flap and was eventually pulled.

Fifteen years later, Calvin Klein pulled yet another campaign because of criticism that the ads portrayed young models in inappropriate situations. Some even likened the campaign to mass-market pedophilia. Klein and others have been criticized for sexualizing young people to sell their brands.

One obvious reason for the criticism is that, for young people, these images are instructive. They see images of people like themselves dressing in a sexually provocative manner and receiving attention. They see images of their peers acting in certain ways and being rewarded with intimacy and romance. In a sense, sexually provocative advertising serves to teach young adults that sex is a prize and that they need only to behave in certain ways to be rewarded. It teaches them what and whom are valued. At the very least, these images and portrayals are an area of concern because they serve as role models for young people.

The Titillation Factor

Young people want to believe that wearing fragrances and certain styles of clothing will help them achieve intimacy by being popular with the opposite sex. For example, an 18-year-old female described the effect Victoria's Secret commercials have on her: "[It] makes me want to go out and buy the product; if these women look good wearing it, so will I." A 21-year-old female who identified a Tommy Hilfiger ad in which a young woman dances seductively in a photo booth, said, "It just put the thought in my mind that it would be fun to dance with my boyfriend like that."

Research also shows that sexual ads are titillating. Ads with sexual information encourage thoughts about sex and about sexual situations. A 20-year-old female, for example, described the effect of a Trojan condom radio ad of a car motor varying at different speeds: "It makes you think about sexual activities and sexual thoughts. With the way the motor sounds, it makes you imagine the different ways and speeds of sexual intercourse."

A 20-year-old male described his reaction to an ad for Wilson's leather goods featuring a female model with her thumbs in the belt loops of her pants: "Just imagining how far she will pull her pants down is a real turn-on."

One female described the mental story she created in response to a Calvin Klein ad: "The wet shiny bodies are very sensual. The hair in the face makes you envision that they just got done with the best lovemaking of their lives and they are so worn out that they don't have enough energy to kiss or put their clothes back on."

Women Are Objectified

Another area of concern is that these ads, as a whole, are sexist. In reality, the vast majority of sexual appeals use images of women to provoke desire. "So what?" a few of my students ask. "Women are naturally more beautiful than men." It may be acceptable for a few isolated incidents, I say, but the cumulative effect of a fairly excessive diet of sexually provocative images of women has been shown to have detrimental effects in regard to attitudes and behaviors about and toward women.

By sexist, it's meant that these images foster stereotypes of social roles based on gender. What stereotypes do these images reinforce? One is that a primary trait or purpose of women is sexual attraction and sexual satisfaction. In these ads, women are present merely to look good and fulfill sexual needs. They also implicitly state that real men have worth when they snare a physically attractive woman. As a whole, these ads devalue vital aspects of the female persona such as personality and intellect.

The message being sent to women is: "You must look like this. You must act like this. You must dress like this. If you want to attract a man or achieve some level of relational 'success' with a man, you need to follow these rules." Similarly, an unspoken set of rules is provided to men: "You need to look for women who look like and behave like this." Are these the scripts we want to instill in our young people?

All this makes sense when you consider that ads for Victoria's Secret were the overall runner-up according to the young adults in the study. Respondents identified Body by

Victoria commercials as well as Angel ads. Interestingly, ads for the Desire campaign by Victoria's Secret were not mentioned. In the ads, Victoria's Secret models Stephanie Seymour and others offer their definitions of "desire." One of them giggles while she says, "Wanting something you can't have," as the camera cuts to a close-up of her breasts.

Sexual Images Cause Disconnection

Sexual images aren't intended to sell us on sex—they are intended to sell us on shopping. The desire they want to inculcate is not for orgasm but for more gismos. This is the intent of the advertisers—but an unintended consequence is the effect these images have on real sexual desire and real lives. When sex is a commodity, there is always a better deal. The wreckage that ensues when people try to emulate the kind of sexuality glorified in the ads and the popular culture is everywhere, from my house to the White House. And many who choose not to act on these impulsive sexual mandates nonetheless end up worrying that something is wrong with them, with their flawed and ordinary and all-too-human relationships. So, all these blatant sexual images that surround us actually are more likely to lead to disconnection rather than to connection.

Jean Kilbourne, in *Sex in Advertising: Perspectives on the Erotic Appeal*, 2003.

Young people picked up on these types of images in Victoria's Secret commercials. According to a 20-year-old female, Victoria's Secret ads are sexy because the models are "hot in nothing but bra and panties." A 20-year-old male said he found Victoria's Secret ads sexy because they contained "half-naked women prancing around."

Obviously, most underwear ads these days tend to show a lot of skin. It is important to remember, though, that they reinforce the sense of implicit sexism discussed above. As argued by feminists and media scholars, these portrayals can influence perceptions of what a woman is, how people behave toward her, and how she perceives of herself.

Consider how a 20-year-old male described an ad for Trojan condoms: "The body of an [apparently] athletic woman with skimpy underwear on and the condom is held up by one of the strings on her panties." Here's why he found the ad to be sexy: "It would have to be a combination of the quite large breasts, toned stomach, and other nice curves without much to cover them up. And when you add the condom, it's like letting you know."

It can work the other way, however. For example, one 19-year-old female described what she found sexy in a commercial for Dentyne's Ice gum: "muscular man—no shirt and tight jeans." One Diet Coke commercial is famous for its role reversal, showing women gawking at a construction worker who sheds his shirt and drinks a Diet Coke during his break. These commercials were created to poke fun at traditional sexist ads, especially those that are sexually oriented.

Corporate and Consumer Backlash

Although truthfulness and substantiation of advertising claims are regulated by law, the "nature" of advertising content is regulated by self-discipline on the part of the ad creator or self-regulated by the advertising profession and media industry. This means that people involved in the process make decisions about what is acceptable based on personal moral considerations, long-term brand positioning considerations, and the desire to avoid negative press and consumer reaction. As a result, brand managers often "kill" ads deemed too risky or provocative. In some instances, networks and local stations refuse to run appeals they consider inappropriate for their viewers or that may violate community standards.

Recently, the publisher of Dallas' *D* magazine reprinted 70,000 issues without a Gucci ad he discovered after the initial press run. In the publisher's opinion, the ad crossed the line of acceptability with regard to blatant sexual imagery.

Consumer backlash can also result in sexual appeals being pulled. One need only think of the Calvin Klein jeans ads, featuring underage models in sexual situations, that were voluntarily pulled after an intense public backlash. Overall, ad professionals claim to have little respect for sexual appeals when used to get attention. To quote one executive, "Whoever created the ad is lazy. Anyone can do it." On the other hand, most agree that, if sex is used in a novel or creative way to communicate brand benefits, or if partnered with humor, it can be very effective.

With their tails tucked between their legs, Jack Valenti, president of the Motion Picture Association of America, and others in the movie industry recently admitted that the practice of promoting films with questionable content to young people is wrong. When one considers reports that consistently show young adults are exposed to thousands of promotional messages every day, many of them containing explicit sexual imagery and innuendo, it is clear that another culprit may be the messenger. Sexual information will be used to sell products as long as people aspire to be sexually attractive to others. Nevertheless, advertisers should be called to task for targeting young people with sexual appeals. Just because it's effective doesn't mean it's right.

"Ad Council programs have shaped American attitudes and behaviors for over 60 years."

Advertisements Provide a Valuable Public Service

Advertising Council

In the following viewpoint the Advertising Council asserts that public-service advertising has made America cleaner and safer. The council details three advertising campaigns that targeted pollution, crime, and drunk driving, and contends that the ads have made people aware of these problems and knowledgeable about their solutions. The Advertising Council is an organization that works with the advertising and communication industries, the media, businesses, and non-profit organizations to take action on important public issues.

As you read, consider the following questions:
1. According to the council, how many Americans belong to neighborhood watch groups?
2. How did the "Take a Bite Out of Crime" campaign help shift people's understanding of crime prevention, as stated by the author?
3. What percentage of adults recognizes the tagline "Friends Don't Let Friends Drive Drunk," according to the council?

Since its earliest days during World War II, the [Advertising] Council has been charged with the mission of identifying a select number of significant public issues and stimulating action on those issues through communications programs that make a measurable difference in our society. We are proud of the fact that the Ad Council is as committed to that mission today as it was at the start, and even prouder that this commitment has generated so many remarkable results.

It is our hope that this [viewpoint] will provide public and social policy leaders, in addition to the public at large, with a living history of how Ad Council programs have shaped American attitudes and behaviors for over 60 years.

Protecting Natural Resources

Most Americans want to help the environment and are eager for easy opportunities to do so. But it wasn't always that way. Long before the environmental movement became mainstream, the Ad Council was in the forefront of educating Americans about the need to take care of our precious resources.

The 1971 Crying Indian campaign:

- Helped usher in Earth Day and the Environmental Protection Agency
- Motivated 100,000 people in the first four months to request a booklet on how to reduce pollution
- Helped reduce litter by as much as 88 percent by 1983
- Is described as one of the 50 greatest commercials

A Distraught Indian

Iron Eyes Cody has lived on in our culture's environmental conscience far longer than the Ad Council ever imagined.

Today, 33 years after the distraught Native American, Iron Eyes Cody, first appeared in an Ad Council public service campaign developed together with Keep America Beautiful (KAB), Inc., a nonprofit that sponsors antilittering initiatives, he is so etched in America's conscience that he continues to act as a solemn reminder of littering and pollution's environmental degradation. Who can forget the disappointed face of the Cherokee Indian atop a horse or in a canoe staring at garbage floating in a pristine river or at trash tossed along the highway?

The sight so dispirited Iron Eyes that it brought a tear to his eye.

"It seems that everyone has seen or heard about the Crying Indian," said Lew Milford, Executive Director of the nonprofit Clean Energy States Alliance. "The Advertising Council's campaign clearly raised the consciousness of people around environmental issues. We had a whole series of environmental issues in the 1960s that were going largely unrecognized. We had virtually no environmental laws to speak of. The Ad Council campaign had some effect on the environmental laws that were ultimately created just by the Crying Indian making people aware of environmental problems."

A Boost to the Environmental Movement

Who can say for sure if the Crying Indian is solely responsible for changing a societal norm? But The Advertising Council, Keep America Beautiful, Inc., and Marsteller, Inc., the agency that developed the campaign pro bono, did play a role in changing how America thought about litter and pollution.

Certainly the famous tear played a role in the fledgling environmental movement and ushering in Earth Day in 1971.

"The tear was such an iconic moment," said Robert Thompson, Director of the Center for the Study of Popular Television at Syracuse University. "It was one of those things that really did become a part of the counterculture. Once you saw it, it was unforgettable. It was like nothing else on television. As such, it stood out in all the clutter we saw in the early '70s."

An Influential Ad

Though it ended in 1983, the Ad Council's campaign is still recognized today. It is one of the most honored ads in advertising history, winning two Clio awards. In addition, *Ad Age* and *TV Guide* described it as one of the 50 greatest commercials. In an online poll, America Online subscribers voted it one of the two best commercials of the century. Today, the TV Land cable network plays it in a series of "retromercials."

"It had a significant impact in actually addressing the issue of litter and getting something done about it," said

G. Raymond Empson, President of Keep America Beautiful, Inc. "For our organization, it fueled a very rapid growth. At the time we were shifting from conducting public awareness messaging exclusively to creating a national network of affiliate organizations that undertook grassroots implementation of our programs to prevent litter. It was an enormous catalyst of that network."

By the time the campaign ended in 1983, Keep America Beautiful reported that its local network had helped reduce litter by as much as 88 percent in 500 communities in 38 states, and even in several countries. . . .

Preventing Crime

Crime is a perennial problem that once seemed too big and inevitable to do anything about. It's just that kind of feeling of helplessness that the Ad Council seeks to change by providing Americans the tools to take charge of their lives and make their communities safe havens, free of crime and fear.

Since McGruff first appeared on the scene:

- Over 75 percent of Americans believe they can do something to stop crime
- More than 20 million Americans belong to Neighborhood Watch groups
- McGruff has become synonymous with friendly, trusted, smart and caring
- He's become a valuable weapon for cash-strapped police departments in delivering crime prevention tips

A Brainstorm at an Airport

The inspiration for one of the Ad Council's most successful public service campaigns came to adman Jack Keil in an airport in Kansas City.

In 1979, a group of law enforcement officers and government agencies, which later formed the National Crime Prevention Council [NCPC], came to the Ad Council seeking a public service campaign to educate Americans on how their involvement can reduce crime. The Ad Council tapped ad agency Dancer Fitzgerald Sample (now Saatchi & Saatchi), where Keil was Creative Director. He understood that people felt vulnerable in the face of rising crime but was at a loss as to how to empower them.

"The attitudes we found in focus groups were that crime is always there and there's nothing we can do about it," said Keil. "This was kind of a downer. Except when we got to the specific question: If there was something simple you could do, would you do it? They said yes. Out of this came a creative strategy that said we can't defeat crime, but we can work against it by taking a lot of little things and putting them together."

Then came the question: how to execute it? On his way home from California, Keil's plane broke down in Kansas City, and he spent hours brainstorming at the airport.

"First I thought of the strategy of little things," recalled Keil. "Maybe we ought to have some sort of cartoon figure like Smokey [the] Bear. Maybe an elephant who would stomp on crime. A lion to roar at crime. Then I went back to what are we trying to get people to do. We are trying to get them to do little things. Take little nips. Bites."

Keil flew out of his seat. Eureka!

"Bite. Bite. Take a bite out of crime!" said Keil, now 81. "Then I instantly thought of a cartoon dog. An animal that takes a bite is a dog."

McGruff's Influence

Thus, 25 years ago in an airport lounge, McGruff the Crime Dog®, a trench-coat-wearing, soulful-looking canine, was born. The ads, which first appeared in 1980, portray McGruff as a wise but warm adviser who can put a paw on your shoulder to reassure you and show you what to do.

Jack Keil's enactment of the McGruff character was so convincing in early presentations that he was unanimously selected to portray McGruff's distinguished voice in all campaign ads. He continues as the voice of McGruff to this day.

McGruff advocates that people take at least small steps like locking doors, leaving lights on at night and enlisting neighbors to watch their houses when away. He promotes safety on the street, at work, at home, in school, in the neighborhood and on the road. The ideas are simple and easy to execute. Anyone can participate just by doing one thing.

McGruff has been instrumental in shifting the paradigm of

crime prevention. "In the early 1970s, people felt it was the police's job to prevent crime," said Jack Calhoun, NCPC's former President and CEO. "Now the polls show that most people feel they can do something and, more important, that they should do something."

The Ad Council and Gun Safety

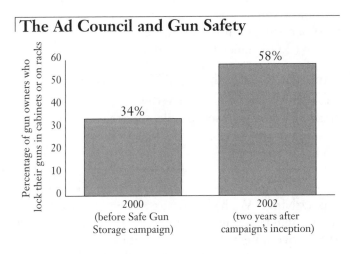

Advertising Council, *Impact of PSA Campaigns*, 2003.

This shift is recognized by experts as helping to turn around many crime statistics. Today, with the campaign's help and over $1.3 billion dollars in donated media since 1980, rather than feeling helpless, more than three out of four Americans believe that they can personally do things to reduce crime. . . .

Preventing Drunk Driving

The Ad Council attempts to change unhealthy or dangerous societal norms. Not too long ago, one norm that we'd all grown accustomed to was the familiar bartime refrain "One more for the road." That phrase is rarely uttered anymore. What's more, keeping drunk drivers off the roads has become a dynamic movement involving young and old, friends and spouses preventing loved ones from driving drunk.

With the help of the Drunk Driving Prevention campaign, begun in 1983:

- The proportion of traffic fatalities caused by alcohol-related crashes has dropped from 60 percent in 1982 to about 45 percent today
- The term "designated driver" is now part of the American vocabulary
- 62 percent of Americans said they tried to stop someone from driving drunk
- 90 percent of adults are aware of the tagline "Friends Don't Let Friends Drive Drunk"

Ending the Acceptability of Drunk Driving

In the early 1980s, the U.S. Department of Transportation realized it had a serious problem on the nation's roads. Something drastic needed to be done.

"What we recognized was that we were losing more than 26,000 people a year in alcohol-related crashes," said John Moulden, President of the National Commission Against Drunk Driving. "We had to figure out what we could possibly do to stem those figures. What transpired was dramatic." In 1982, government data showed that 60 percent of all traffic fatalities were caused by intoxicated drivers.

In 1983, when Moulden worked with the National Highway Traffic Safety Administration (NHTSA)—charged with reducing traffic injuries—the agency asked The Advertising Council for help. NHTSA badly needed a national strategy to reach a country that saw drinking and driving as socially acceptable.

"One of the ways we thought about changing behavior was through advertising," said Kathryn Henry, a Program Analyst who joined NHTSA 12 years ago. "It's the best way to reach a majority of the people."

NHTSA's request nicely dovetailed with The Advertising Council's mission to create powerful advertising to solve important public issues. The strategy is often the same. Educate Americans about a serious societal problem it faces and encourage a necessary change in behavior. It assigned the first spots to the ad agency Leber Katz Partners, which later was absorbed into Foote Cone & Belding.

As with all preliminary Ad Council campaigns, research was conducted to help inform the campaign strategy and outside studies were scrutinized. One particular study by Harvard University indicated it would be more effective to target a drunk driver's spouse and friends because they're in the best position to take away the keys.

"The original campaign was a real breakthrough," said Ruth Wooden, President of The Advertising Council from 1987 to 1999. "Instead of going after the drunk driver, the strategy was to try to direct the message to the person who could stop someone from driving drunk. It's called the Intervener Strategy. It's absolutely brilliant."

The initiative also became the progenitor for the designated driver—another breakthrough concept where the driver agrees to not drink. Bartenders and restaurants still offer free food and sodas to encourage designated drivers. Nobody had ever talked about designated drivers before this campaign.

Soon "Friends Don't Let Friends Drive Drunk" was replacing "One More for the Road." The ads were practical. They accepted that people will drink but advocated that if they down a few Scotches, let someone else drive. The early ads were edgy. Wine glasses or beer mugs were raised high in a toast. Instead of the expected sound of glasses clinking, brakes screech and glass shatters in a deadly crash. "You talk to college kids today and they use designated drivers. It's just something most people do. We've made a real impact," said Ad Council President and CEO Peggy Conlon.

The ads were effective. A 2002 Ad Council survey showed that 90 percent of adults were aware of advertising with the tagline "Friends Don't Let Friends Drive Drunk."

Reducing Fatalities

The Ad Council doesn't take sides or push for legislation. But experts say the campaign inspired legislative changes. Soon politicians enacted tough state laws setting a strict allowable blood alcohol content.

The ads had another effect. By 1993, the percentage of traffic fatalities due to alcohol-related automobile crashes had dropped to 45 percent, from 60 percent in 1982. "The period between 1981 and the mid-1990s was marked by an unprecedented downturn in drunk driving deaths," said John Moulden, who has worked on this issue since 1972. "Those of us who've been in the field a long time were astounded by the tremendous reduction. It showed we really could reduce the number of drunk driving deaths."

A norm had been changed. "It became socially unaccept-able to drive drunk," said Moulden. "The norm shifted from seeing drunk driving as only a social faux pas, but everybody still does it, to recognizing the horrible consequences to real people. The ads gave people a sense that they could do something about it by really playing on the intervener role."

Periodical Bibliography

The following articles have been selected to supplement the diverse views presented in this chapter.

David Benady	"Playing Fairer with Sex?" *Marketing Week*, August 5, 2004.
Kate Clinton	"Tastefully Gay," *Progressive*, September 2000.
Rance Crain	"Husbands Are Boys and Wives Their Mothers in the Land of Ads," *Advertising Age*, March 26, 2001.
Michael Haas	"Gay Ads Turn on TV Viewers," *Genre*, September 2001.
Tristram Hunt	"Kick the Advertisements Out," *New Statesman*, December 16, 2002.
Issues and Controversies On File	"Prescription Drug Advertising," June 8, 2001.
Patrick Marshall	"Advertising Overload," *CQ Researcher*, January 23, 2004.
Jonathan M. Metzl	"Selling Sanity Through Gender," *Ms.*, Fall 2003.
Russell Mokhiber and Robert Weissman	"Advertise This!" *Progressive Populist*, October 1, 2002.
Kate Peirce	"What If the Energizer Bunny Were Female?" *Sex Roles*, December 2001.
Deana A. Rohlinger	"Eroticizing Men," *Sex Roles*, February 2002.
Joan Voight	"Don't Box Me In," *Brandweek*, September 1, 2003.

CHAPTER 2

Does Advertising Exploit Children?

Chapter Preface

In 1990 a news program geared to adolescents began broadcasting in four hundred schools. Called Channel One, the program provided schools with audio-visual equipment if they agreed to broadcast twelve minutes of Channel One programming each day. Ten of those minutes were devoted to news, while the remaining minutes consisted of commercials. Advertising directed at children has historically spawned intense debate, and Channel One ads are no exception.

Critics of Channel One charge that the company is taking advantage of the fact that it has a captive audience—U.S. children are required to attend school. Moreover, unlike when they are watching television at home, students cannot switch the channel or turn the television off when a commercial airs. Pat Ellis, writing for *Education Reporter*, asserts, "We understand that the purpose of advertising is to manipulate our wants and desires. What we don't understand is why so many educators don't have a problem with exploiting a captive audience of children in this way." According to Ellis, these exploitative advertisements include commercials for violent rap music groups and movies that may be inappropriate for teenagers. Furthermore, many critics contend that these commercials can devalue education. Elizabeth Bauchner, in an article for the *Ithaca Journal*, opines, "Schools are supposed to be a place for learning. What are we teaching our children by mandating they watch commercials?"

On the other hand, Channel One and its supporters maintain that the company provides a valuable service and does not exploit children. While some critics contend that the ten minutes of news programming contains little hard news, Channel One points to the numerous awards its programming has received, including a Peabody Award in 1992 for its series on AIDS. Its supporters include Amy Ridenour, the president of the National Center for Public Policy Research. In her commentary "Activists Take Aim at Corporate Involvement in Schools," Ridenour asserts that the value of programming and equipment provided by Channel One far outweigh the potentially negative effects of two minutes of commercials. She notes that Channel One is a voluntary program—if schools believe their students are being exploited, they can end their agreements with the company. However, Ridenour writes, the negative view some people have of Channel One "does not seem to be echoed by the schools who have tried Channel One, as 99% of the schools that subscribe to the service have been choosing to continue their subscriptions."

Whether at school, on television, in magazines, or through other media, advertising influences children. These commercials can positively or negatively impact the values, behavior, and spending habits of the nation's youth. In the following chapter the authors consider whether advertising exploits children or if its impact has been misunderstood.

"For the past decade, corporations have feasted upon kids like jackals at a carcass."

Advertising Is Harmful to Children

Roy F. Fox

In the following viewpoint Roy F. Fox contends that advertising is harmful to the physical and social health of children. He argues that the thousands of commercials seen by children each year cause obesity and other health problems by encouraging the consumption of soda, candy, and high-fat foods. Furthermore, Fox maintains, advertisements help children develop negative values such as materialism and instant gratification. He concludes that schools, governments, and professional organizations must take steps to reduce the effects of advertising on children. Fox is a professor of education at the University of Missouri at Columbia and the author of *Harvesting Minds: How TV Commercials Control Kids.*

As you read, consider the following questions:

1. According to the author, how much money do American advertisers spend each year?
2. How much more soda than milk do teenagers drink, according to a report cited by Fox?
3. As stated by an article cited by Fox, African American children view how many television commercials each year?

Roy F. Fox, "Warning: Advertising May Be Hazardous to Your Health: Ads Pose a Threat to Physical, Emotional, Social, and Cultural Well-Being," *USA Today Magazine*, November 2001. Copyright © 2001 by the Society for the Advancement of Education. Reproduced by permission.

Each year, American advertisers spend approximately $150,000,000,000—a cost that is passed on to consumers in higher prices. As consumers, our relationship with advertisers is a curious one. We pay for the cost of advertising and supply the profits. We also pay for the total tax write-off that businesses receive for advertising expenses. A large sign inside Russia's Mir space station before it was destroyed summed it all up: "Even in Space . . . Pepsi Is Changing the Script." Indeed, advertising seems like the only script around—on Earth as it is in heaven.

Consumption—and the advertising that drives it—is our most powerful cultural force, shaping our attitudes, beliefs, values, and lifestyles. Pervasive and powerful, advertising's effects largely go unseen, because we think about advertising like fish think about water—we don't. This is especially true for children and young adults, who have grown up immersed in a world that promises everything, to everyone, all the time —for a price. Because kids are a potential long-term investment, advertisers position them as "super targets."

The Move to Target Children

In the 1960s, marketers began to define children as a separate demographic category. By the late 1970s, research indicated that children had trouble distinguishing between television programs and commercials. Most had little or no understanding of ads' persuasive intentions, thus making them highly vulnerable to commercial claims and appeals. In 1978, such research prompted the Federal Trade Commission to attempt to ban TV commercials aimed at youngsters.

Ironically, the trend to marketing to kids gained momentum, culminating in the establishment of Channel One [a news network geared to teenagers] in 1989, which now beams television commercials to a captive audience of more than 8,000,000 students in 40% of America's schools. One of my own studies in 1996 found that students attending Channel One schools reconstruct or "replay" the ads, creating a kind of "echo chamber" for their messages. This study found that many of the items advertised on Channel One are sold within the schools. One advertising executive stated, "You've got to reach kids throughout the day—in school, as they're shopping in the mall . . . or at the movies. You've got to become part of the fabric of their lives." This trend will gain momentum as technology, marketing research, and electronic media become ever more sophisticated at invading students' lives—at home, play, or school.

Market researchers now work directly in some schools to determine "what sparks kids." One company conducts focus groups in school on behalf of KFC, McDonalds, and Mattel Toys—all to improve advertising to kids. To date, the most ambitious marketing venture is ZapMe! Corporation's offer of entire computer labs, fast servers with satellite connection, teacher training, and other hi-tech lollipops to public and private schools—all "free." The only price is that the systems contain ads—in all their interactive and multimedia glories. ZapMe! folks, though, don't call this advertising. Instead, what they call it is "brand imaging spots" and "dedicated branding spaces."

About 9,000 schools signed up. Although ZapMe! filed bankruptcy, another entrepreneur will likely continue what is already entrenched. The ZapMe! approach is strikingly similar to Channel One television. In exchange for delivering this massive audience, schools receive monitors, a satellite dish (only capable of picking up Channel One's signal), and other equipment amounting to about $50,000. Hence, Channel One is found most often in low-income communities.

Few Benefits, Many Problems

One "benefit" of beaming Channel One television into classrooms is supposed to be its news program. However, research has concluded that this contains precious little news. The bulk of each broadcast (80% according to one study) is devoted to advertising, sports, weather, and natural disasters, features and profiles, and self-promotion of Channel One.

The president of ZapMe! told researcher Dawn Chmielewski that "Channel One is television. What we are is really an interactive learning tool, so we're very, very different." Of course, the Internet differs from TV. We long have known that, when people interact with texts, they improve their retention and learning, internalizing those messages more quickly and deeply. ZapMe! used this power to sell stuff.

Students were further immersed in ad-culture when they collected "ZapPoints," which they spent at an e-commerce mall. The constantly moving billboard on the screen and the coupons were not the worst thing, though. The ZapMe! technology also monitored students' movements on the computers, then sold this data to market research firms.

Both Channel One and ZapMe! fail to allow teachers or administrators access to the material delivered to students. Teachers cannot preview Channel One's daily broadcasts, since the signals are received inside of a locked, metal box, and nobody at the schools has a key to open it. Nor can schools alter the ZapMe! web browser. Such is the state of democratic education—an institution founded to resist such influences. . . .

Harmful to Children's Health

Ads for junk food, tobacco, and liquor encourage unhealthy choices. In 1998, researchers found that TV commercials lowered children's ability to resist the temptation for low-nutrition food. This was 15 years after a study which concluded that sports celebrities in TV and magazine ads promoting the use of snuff and chewing tobacco led to increased numbers of young people using these products. Other research found that ads for alcohol became "increasingly salient and attractive [to kids] between the ages of 10 and 14 years."

In 1994, the American Academy of Pediatrics adopted strong policies opposing advertising to children. The Academy estimates that, each year, youngsters are exposed to 2,000 television ads for beer and wine. It believes that this may explain the increase in kids' liquor consumption. Moreover, the Academy contends that the increase in children's obesity correlates with youngsters watching more TV commercials that tout foods high in salt, sugar, and fat.

Sugared drinks or "liquid candy" are a major concern today. According to a report by the Center for Science in the Public Interest, teenagers of 20 years ago "were drinking almost twice as much milk as soda pop . . . now they're drinking twice as much soda pop as milk." What results is the systematic destruction of physical health through increases in obesity, cardiovascular disease, lowered bone mass and osteoporosis (especially in women), tooth decay, heart disease, kidney stones, Type II diabetes, and more. Any consideration of physical health should include the social and psychological difficulties that often accompany and intensify physical illnesses, sometimes even generating new ones. For example, diabetic children may feel embarrassed when they have to leave the classroom in order to take insulin or remedy a low blood-sugar level. This, in turn, may elicit "coping" attitudes and behaviors that would not have otherwise developed.

Sodas in Schools

Since the 1950s, we have been conditioned to down more and more sweet soda. During that decade, standard soda containers held 6.5 ounces. Next came the 12-ounce can. Today, the line of massive machines in my campus office building—machines that are seductively curved, like that luscious bottle—sell only the 20-ounce size. Fast food outlets and convenience stores offer special deals for the "Double Gulp." I doubt, though, if most people can down 64 ounces in two swallows.

Coca-Cola, Pepsi, and other brands are vigorously marketed in schools, hawked endlessly to captive audiences who must watch glitzy commercials as part of the school's contract with Channel One. Soft drinks are marketed on the Internet, on stadium scoreboards, in school hallways, on clothing, and on book covers. Ads in schools can "legitimize" the products. As one student told me, "Why would it be here if they [teachers, administrators, parents] didn't think it was good for us?" School districts often sign multi-million-dollar contracts with soft drink companies, which seek exclusive "pouring rights." The Houston district signed a contract with Coke, worth more than $5,000,000 over five years (and this is the district once managed by Secretary of Education Rod Paige). Dentists and others have noted that Pepsi, Dr. Pepper, and Seven-Up sell the use of their logos to a large producer of baby bottles, the Munchkin Bottling Company. Dentists estimate that infants and toddlers are four times likelier to be fed soda out of those bottles than out of regular baby bottles.

In part, this is because youngsters now have more money to spend and more influence over how their parents' money is spent. Add to this the marketers' quest to establish "brand name loyalty" as early in children's lives as possible. Consequently, advertising—from cradle to grave—fills the air. At this rate, soda machines in schools will crowd out computers, and playground equipment will become climbable Pepsi dispensers. . . .

Encouraging Materialism

Advertisers bombard us with powerful messages reflecting values, attitudes, and ideologies that are not always conducive to social and environmental health. These include, but are not limited to, valuing appearance over substance, instant gratification over delayed gratification, action over reflection, consumption over frugality and recycling, competition over cooperation, and materialism over spirituality.

Advertising Readily Influences Children

Does advertising affect children's commercial recall and product preferences? If not, the $12 billion spent annually by advertisers in commercial appeals to children would represent a surprisingly poor investment. . . .

Research on children's commercial recall and product preferences confirms that advertising typically achieves its intended effects. A variety of studies using differing methodologies find that children recall content from the ads to which they've been exposed. Product preference has been shown to occur with as little as a single commercial exposure and to strengthen with repeated exposures. Most importantly, studies have shown that product preferences affect children's product purchase requests and that these requests do influence parents' purchasing decisions.

Report of the American Psychological Association Task Force on Advertising and Children, February 20, 2004.

In the 1950s, British children who watched television (the BBC, which contained no commercials) developed more materialistic attitudes than those who did not. According to Patricia M. Greenfield's *Mind and Media: The Effects of Television, Video Games, and Computers,* "Adolescent boys who watched television . . . were more focused on what they would have in the future, adolescent boys without television were more focused on what they would be doing. The longer the child's experience with television, the more this materialistic outlook increased." This problem seems more severe with low-income, African-American children. According to *Psychiatric Forum*, they view "significantly more TV than whites . . . an average of 6.85 hours of TV each day and 40,000 TV commercials each year." The result is that "Black families overspend in the attempt to be like the persons depicted in TV commercials."

Materialism involves more than just a belief in objects for objects' sake or "keeping up with the Joneses." It presents the view that intangible qualities, such as sex appeal or popularity, can be obtained by purchasing a product, such as a soft drink. Researchers Bradley Greenberg and J.E. Brand concluded that Channel One viewers held "more materialistic attitudes" than nonviewers. Others found that ads not only encouraged youngsters to adopt materialistic attitudes, but generated friction between parents and children, limiting the development of kids' moral and ethical values.

Consider the Temple of Nike ad, which, many would agree, mocks and trivializes the traditional source of moral and ethical values—the place of worship. This ad's glowing yellows, reds, blues, greens, and purples add realism to the stained glass windows of the praying sports stars. The different balls from the various sports serve as halos around each sports god. The line of small print that states "Hours of worship Mon–Sat 10–7 P.M. Thurs 10–8 P.M. Sun 11–6 P.M." clinches the message that sports are holy and, since Nike is sports, Nike must be holy. Other, "larger" messages evolve from this ad: That what is holier than sports and even holier than Nike is spending money; that no entity outside of ourselves is bigger than basketball star Michael Jordan; and that those who adopt the stance of prayer—the most private and vulnerable of human acts—are fair game for exploitation. . . .

Six Steps to Take

Deeply embedded in our social and cultural history, advertising is so prevalent that it is invisible. Nevertheless, there is plenty for us to do. For starters, we can train teachers in media literacy. Second, we can support new technology that will allow viewers to skip television commercials.

Third, we can establish "ad-free zones" in schools, places of worship, and other public spaces that have natural, architectural, historical, or cultural value. Federal legislation is needed to ban print and electronic advertising, now commonplace in most schools. After all, the American school was founded to be a marketplace of ideas—not a marketplace of products and packaged ideologies wrapped in the guise of entertaining TV ads and programs. Fourth, if ads can't be banned wholesale in schools, the next-best solution is to impose heavy taxes on them.

Fifth, professional organizations should develop and enforce codes of ethics. For example, psychologists often use their training in human behavior to design more effective advertising aimed at children. Research methods, such as focus groups, are often designed to lay bare kids' fears, dreams, desires, and fantasies. These young "subjects" are unaware that they are being manipulated. However, the American Psychiatric Association's Code of Conduct does not even address this issue.

Finally, we can support nonprofit groups that advocate media education, such as Commercial Alert, based in Washington, D.C., and The Cultural Environment Movement, a coalition of independent organizations and individuals from every U.S. state and 57 countries on six continents.

"It . . . seems both pessimistic and disrespectful to dismiss the current generation of teens as 'branded for life.'"

Advertising Is Not Harmful to Children

Elizabeth Austin

Commercials do not turn adolescents into mindless materialists, Elizabeth Austin opines in the following viewpoint. According to Austin, children are not helpless victims who need government protection from villainous corporations. Austin claims that today's children are no more vulnerable to advertising's lures than were children of previous generations. Austin is a journalist and author.

As you read, consider the following questions:

1. Why does Austin believe it is more difficult for advertisers to influence today's children than it was to have an impact on previous generations?
2. In the author's view, how does Alissa Quart misinterpret the lessons of several popular teenage movies?
3. According to Austin, how does the television cartoon *Daria* prove that teenagers are not slaves to corporations and commercials?

A lissa Quart believes that kids today are victims of an un-precedented barrage of slick, mind-numbing advertising, a phenomenon dissected at length in her book *Branded: The Buying and Selling of Teenagers*. To check her thesis, I called a 40-something friend and asked if she remembered which brand of sneakers she wore as a child. My friend burst into song: "Run a little faster, jump a little higher, feel a little stronger, in your P.F. Flyers!"

I was stunned; I'd always thought of her as a Red Ball Jets girl. But I wasn't surprised that the insistent commercial jingles of her childhood remained embedded in her brain. It's hard to imagine a baby boomer who doesn't know which brand of chicken noodle soup is "M'm! M'm! Good," what kind of bread builds strong bodies 12 ways, or why Tony the Tiger starts every morning with sugar-frosted flakes. (For you youngsters out there, it's because they're "Grrrrrrr-eat!") It's certainly true that children today are bombarded by commercial messages in a way that was unimaginable back when there were only three networks, and children spent each endless week waiting breathlessly for the glories of Saturday morning cartoons.

But it's an open question whether Nickelodeon, Cartoon Network, the Disney Channel, and their ilk have made today's children more vulnerable to commercialism than their parents were. With so much kid-oriented programming available, no current shows can boast the hegemony—and commercial muscle—of old must-see juvenile hits like "Batman" or "The Monkees"; advertisers on those shows knew that every self-respecting third-grader in the country would either tune in or face playground humiliation the next day. It's impossible for an advertiser to make that kind of direct hit in today's cluttered media marketplace.

Blaming the Wrong People

Children, Quart argues, have been transformed into "victims of the contemporary luxury economy." To her, the villains in this case are obvious: They are the corporations that heartlessly market to underage consumers, slavering after the annual $155 billion in discretionary income Quart says they control (although the source of that figure is not cited).

Some of her anecdotal evidence is chilling, such as the 150 school districts nationwide that have accepted soft-drink companies' sponsorships, taking relatively small donations in return for exclusive on-campus access to the districts' thirsty young customers. Quart reports that one young rebel who wore a Pepsi shirt to his school's Coca-Cola Day was suspended for "insurrection."

Still, isn't criticizing a marketer for targeting a group of affluent consumers, whatever their height, equivalent to deploring your cat for targeting songbirds? It's in the nature of the beast. The real challenge is deciding whose job it is to bell the cat. Quart blames Congress for its failure to regulate advertising to under-18 consumers. She notes with approval that Sweden bans commercials on kids' shows, a move that demonstrates that "many European countries are much more enlightened than the United States in their attitudes and laws toward branding aimed at minors." But that's a spurious comparison. Unlike the United States, where commercial jingles and slogans have been part of the cultural fabric for more than half a century, Sweden didn't allow any commercials on television whatsoever until 1991. (That ban had one unexpectedly lovely unintended consequence. Marketers, desperate to get buyers' attention, started plastering their brand logos on brightly colored hot-air balloons and setting them aloft over Stockholm.) And the current ban on marketing to kids doesn't actually work; to circumvent it, two Swedish channels simply beam their signals from ad-friendlier England.

The author seems to put more faith in legislative action than in parents' own ability to monitor their children's exposure to advertising and limit their purchasing power. Sadly, she may be right. Many parents, whether motivated by guilt or wrong-headed fondness, seem unable to resist their children's demands for expensive branded merchandise, even when those desires wreak havoc on the family budget. A few days ago, I was minding the cash register at our elementary-school book fair when a distressed single mother asked me to total her purchases. She had planned to spend only $60, but her son's wish list totaled almost $100. I offered to take back the most expensive volume, a $28 hardcover version of the Guinness Book of World Records. "It'll be out in paperback soon," I assured her. "He wants what he wants," she responded flatly, digging in her purse for a few more crumpled bills. How can we expect our children to build up any sales resistance when we ourselves are unable to say no?

A Distorted View

Although it's easy to share Quart's indignation about the branding of America's littlest consumers, it's unfortunate that her ire sometimes distorts her vision of popular culture. Her chapter on recent teen films proves that it's possible to delve so far into subtext that you can miss the text entirely. In bemoaning the lack of "responsible, liberal reflexes" in today's teen movies, she takes aim at *Bring It On*, *Legally Blonde*, and a token brunette movie, *She's All That*—a trio of warm-hearted, if featherweight flicks. In [Quart's] view, these films celebrate "influencers"—better known as "the cool kids"—to the detriment of everybody else.

How Children Relate Their Positive Self-Image to Their Favorite Clothing Brands

Here's what kids said that tells us to what extent their self-image is tied up in the brands they wear:

- I am brave and confident.
- It shows my attitude.
- I'm excited about myself.
- I like to skateboard and that's what's on the shirt.
- Show-off.
- 'Cause I just want to do lots of things.
- I think I am pretty.
- I like to joke around lots.
- Because I'm always nice.
- I like to play sports lots.
- I have no worries.
- It's kind of smart-aleck.
- I like to play.
- It's all about me!

Martin Lindstrom, *Brandchild*, 2003.

But while it's true that the stars of these films are all substantially more physically attractive than, say, your average

Miss America contestant, the plots of these movies all turn on the value of personal integrity over social acceptance. Even though these films are all so sugary they should have carried a warning to diabetic viewers, they're hardly evil. (Indeed, Quart distorts the most memorable line in *She's All That*. After the teen Galatea[1] turns her back on high-end prom culture, she returns to her loving middle-class home to find her smitten young Pygmalion patiently waiting for her. As he draws her close in the warm, starry California night, she breathes: "I feel just like Julia Roberts in *Pretty Woman*—except for that whole hooker thing." Indefensibly, Quart cuts out that last, knowing phrase.)

Idealistic and Anti-Materialistic

It's a shame that Quart chooses to stack her deck, because she raises some interesting points about current teen culture and the adult marketers who have so effectively plugged into it. In her chapter on peer-to-peer marketing, she reports on the growing army of enthusiastic teens who cheerfully volunteer massive amounts of time to help their favorite brands reach other young consumers. These un- and underpaid teens believe their efforts eventually will be rewarded by cool jobs in fashion and marketing. While Quart tsks that the corporate adults who recruit these easily exploited young people "do not have the kids' interests at heart" (there's that carnivorous cat problem again), it's more interesting to wonder how nobler organizations might use these marketers' techniques to harness these kids' energy, hope, and idealism.

It also seems both pessimistic and disrespectful to dismiss the current generation of teens as "branded for life." Sure, if you walk through your local mall, you're likely to see more brand names displayed on young bodies than in the store windows. But there are also signs that this generation of kids is savvier than Quart believes. As evidence, take a look at "Daria," a teen-oriented cartoon about a young, suburban Dorothy Parker[2] in combat boots. Smart, sarcastic, and so-

1. Referring to the legend of Galatea, a statue by the sculptor Pygmalion. Pygmalion fell in love with Galatea, whom the goddess Aphrodite brought to life. 2. Parker was a literary critic and writer known for her sarcasm and wit. She wrote mostly during the 1920s and 1930s.

cially aware, Daria repeatedly proves herself more than able to fend off the dark forces of marketing and materialism. When Lawndale High's principal sells the school's soul to Ultra Cola for a cool 50 grand, Daria takes action to get (most of) the company's intrusive ads removed from the hall-ways—and the curriculum. And when Val, the editor of an eponymous teen magazine, tries to exploit Daria as a one-girl focus group, the cynical teen denounces her as an oppor-tunist and advises her to start helping young women with their problems, instead of adding to them. From 1997 until its final episode in 2001, "Daria" was a favorite of both so-phisticated anti-corporate teens and the Abercrombie & Fitch wearers the show so gleefully lampooned. (In 1999, *Teen People* gave "Daria" a Readers' Choice award.) And which pioneering, anti-materialist pro-feminist network dared to create this intelligent, subversive show? MTV. Go figure.

"*The more corporate special interests are allowed to influence what schools teach . . . the less students are seen as active citizens-to-be and rather as passive consumers-to-be-sold.*"

Advertising in Schools Gives Corporations Too Much Influence

Alex Molnar

In the following viewpoint Alex Molnar asserts that advertising in schools has left students vulnerable to corporate values that run counter to the goals of public education. According to Molnar, commercialism in schools can take many forms. For example, incentive programs offer an award of a company product for specific academic achievements. Other corporations actually help shape the curriculum by donating educational materials friendly to their business goals. Through these actions American companies are shaping what U.S. students learn. Molnar is the director of the Education Policy Studies Laboratory at Arizona State University.

As you read, consider the following questions:

1. According to Molnar, how has the No Child Left Behind Act affected commercialism in schools?
2. What is "appropriation of space," as defined by the author?

Alex Molnar, *Virtually Everywhere: Marketing to Children in America's Schools: The Seventh Annual Report on Schoolhouse Commercialism Trends, 2003–2004*, Educational Policy Studies Laboratory, Commercialism in Education Research Unit, 2004. Copyright © 2004 by the Educational Policy Studies Laboratory. Reproduced by permission.

The spread of schoolhouse commercialism is part of a much broader trend, the encroachment of commercial interests into every element of modern culture. What sets it apart is the way it subjects children to its influence. And children are increasingly the prime target audience for corporations seeking to sell. As a sign of how important the youth market is to advertisers, consider that organizations such as Alloy Inc., and its subsidiary, 360 Youth, exist solely to market to teens. Alloy is a media, direct marketing and marketing services company targeting the audience ranging in age from 10 to 24. Alloy's media and marketing arm, 360 Youth, targets teens and college-age people with in-school billboards, high school and college newspapers, websites, magazines, and catalogues. Meanwhile, cable television viewing by children has reached record levels—cable accounts for 68 percent of children's daily TV watching—and advertisers are flocking to the shows they watch to sell them products.

New Opportunities for Commercialism

Schools have become integral to the marketing plans of a vast array of corporations. "What we have now is an ingrained idea that public schools exist for private profit," observed Georgia State University education professor Deron Boyles.

Schoolhouse commercialism entails selling *to* schools, selling *in* schools, and finally, the selling *of* schools and of education as a marketable commodity. Although selling to schools is nearly as old as common schools themselves, even in that traditional arena, new developments have been surfacing. The passage of the No Child Left Behind Act [NCLB], imposing test-performance and other mandates on schools as a condition of receiving federal aid, has given suppliers new marketing opportunities. Microsoft, Excelsior Software, Blackboard Inc., Plato Learning, and other suppliers of products that schools use have, in various ways, promoted their wares as helping schools meet the demands of NCLB. In an address to securities analysts in January 2004, Raymond Marchuk, a senior executive from the publisher Scholastic Inc., noted that his company expected to see its educational publishing segment grow 10 percent over its original target thanks in part to the pressure on schools to raise reading scores under NCLB. (Poking fun at the trend, a desk maker is reported to have put up a sign at a school board convention touting its furniture as "No Child Left Behind-compliant."). . .

Incentive Programs Offer Further Opportunities for Commercialism

Incentive programs provide some sort of reward in the form of a commercial product or service in return for students who achieve an ostensibly academic goal, such as perfect attendance or increased reading. Media references to such programs were essentially flat, dropping by about 0.8 percent to 351 in the 2003–2004 [school year], from 354 references in the 2002–2003 [school year].

Pizza Hut's "Book It" program offers children free pizza for achieving certain reading goals, and adds to its program by bringing celebrities into classrooms to read to students on November 11, National Young Readers Day. McDonald's provides a variety of incentives, the rewards being for the fast-food giant's products. The AMC Theatres chain of movie houses offers children free concessions for reading three books. The Six Flags chain of amusement parks offers free admission to children who maintain a log, monitored by adults, indicating they have read a total of 360 minutes worth of material during the school year. Papa John's Pizza outlets give schools "Winner's Circle" cards for free pizza, donuts, ice cream, video games, and museum visits, to be distributed to students who earn all Cs or better on report cards. In Houston, Texas, students who attain perfect attendance records are rewarded with packs of National Football League player trading cards, posters, and other pro-football booty. The program, which focuses each year on the city designated to host the Super Bowl, is sponsored by makers of sports trading cards. . . .

The end result of such incentive programs contributes to a shifting view of education from a collective, public good that engages the next generation in the American civic life to an individual, private good that becomes another consumer product and thereby helps reinforce a consumerist ideology. Thus a suggestion in *Forbes*—issued in all apparent sincerity—becomes completely unsurprising: Edward Miguel, writing in the November 24, 2003, issue of the business magazine, argues that students should be awarded cash for scoring high on standardized tests, and contends examples from Kenya, Israel, and the United Kingdom demonstrate that such a policy can lift achievement. Even students who did not qualify for the incentives lifted their scores, Miguel claimed.

Appropriation of Space

Appropriation of Space is the use of school property to promote individual corporations through mechanisms such as naming rights or general advertising. References in this category rose by 87 percent, to 611 references in 2003–2004 from 326 in 2002–2003. Since 1990, such references have risen 394 percent.

Advertising is pervasive in schools. In December 2003, Marvel Enterprises acquired Cover Concepts from Hearst Communications. Cover Concepts distributes book covers, coloring books, posters, and calendars in 43,000 public schools; the materials are laden with ads, and Marvel in making the acquisition said it hoped the deal "will widen its exposure to a younger demographic" while also helping the comic book maker "keep its classic comic characters current and hip with the audience that matters most to filmmakers and toy sellers."

One recurring theme in this category for the year under study was school bus advertising. Growing numbers of schools made plans to raise money by selling ads on school buses, either to be seen by the youthful riders or by members of the public passing by. Plans were approved or proposals made in Lee County, Florida, Braintree, Beverly, and Plymouth, Massachusetts, Lake Oswego, Oregon, Tulsa, Oklahoma, and Miami-Dade County, Florida, among other communities. Not all bus ad programs succeeded, however. In Putnam County, Florida, a school bus ad agency signed a contract expecting 13 neighboring counties to sign on as well. They did not, leaving the agency with too small a base to lure big-ticket ads from companies like Tropicana, Dole and Office Depot.

Advertising is not limited to buses. Scoreboards with corporate logos have been another popular advertising medium. Game programs are a long-standing vehicle for such ads. Occasionally, however, school advertising backfires, as when a Catholic school in Pittsburgh published in its girls' high school basketball program an ad for a provider of exotic dancers. The ad touted the dancers' services for, among other things, divorce parties. "Everyone involved in this is totally embarrassed by it," said a spokesperson for the Pittsburgh Catholic Diocese. . . .

Commercialism in the Curriculum

For corporations to provide curriculum materials directly related to their industries is inherently problematic, risking that students will receive distorted or self-serving messages. Consider, for example, the "Pick Protein" curriculum, distributed by the Weekly Reader Corp. "to teach students in grades 9–12 about choosing a healthy lifestyle." Co-sponsors of the curriculum are America's Pork Producers, the trade group for pork-product marketers. The material "encourages students to consider what they eat, and to make informed choices, including lean protein sources such as pork, as an important part of a healthy lifestyle."

The Pressures of Consumerism

We have all become inured to the constant barrage of advertising, but for me, consumerism is a real problem. The pressure to buy and to measure our success in life through the things we acquire is overwhelming. Education should offer a way for students to seek a good life that means more than just wealth. It saddens me to see our schools become part of this marketing machinery. Public schools should be a respite from the constant onslaught of advertisers.

John Sheehan, *American School Board Journal*, October 1999.

Parents and teachers alike should have every reason to question whether the material provides a full, complete and balanced appraisal of, for example, the health benefits of a vegetarian diet, or the conditions under which pigs are raised and their meat is processed. Similar questions might be raised about whether McDonald's free elementary school nutrition program "What's on your Plate"—teaching "the importance of physical activity and making smart food choices"—inappropriately diverts classroom discussion from the high fat, sugar, and sodium content of the fast-food purveyor's products.

Some programs would appear to be little more than advertising, such as the "Elf study guides in the shape of toys" being distributed to 10,000 schools by New Line Cinema in advance of the release of its film *Elf* in late 2003. Other programs may impart some genuine value—along with free advertising for the sponsor. In Florida, BankAtlantic distributed a math workbook to elementary school students with math problems with a banking theme—not incidentally building name recognition with the youngsters. Court TV won an industry promotion award for its "Forensics in the Classroom" curriculum, which "built public support for science in schools —and won itself millions of brand impressions.". . .

Promoting Values

Some corporate curriculum materials do not necessarily relate directly to the company's products, but are intended to promote a company's cultural values. For instance, MassMutual Financial Group and its Oppenheimer Funds unit sponsor an "educational outreach program" for middle-school children, in use in 2,500 classrooms, that focuses on "character education" and offers "lessons on tolerance, body image, diversity and teamwork."

Chick-fil-A, a fast-food chain that articulates its "statement of corporate purpose" as "to glorify God by being a faithful steward of all that is entrusted to us and to have a positive influence on all who come in contact with Chick-fil-A," gives a "Core Essentials" character-education curriculum to 1,100 elementary schools around the country, reaching, by its own count, 575,000 students a year. The company also has incentive programs for reading and attendance in schools with which it forms partnerships, and gives out books on partnership with public television's reading show, "Between the Lions.". . .

Public Education Is Losing Its Meaning

Uncovering and scrutinizing the influence of corporations in public schools forces us, ultimately, to grapple with the question of what our schools are for. The American ideal of public education has historically been conceived as a means for preparing the next generation to participate fully in a free and democratic society—a role that requires responsible questioning of the status quo and of established power structures. The more corporate special interests are allowed to influence what schools teach—and, by extension, limit what they cannot teach—the less students are seen as active citizens to be and rather as passive consumers to be sold the farther our educational system moves from that ideal.

| *"Commercialism in schools can provide great advantages for students, staff, parents, and the public."*

Advertising in Schools Can Be Justified

William C. Bosher Jr., Kate R. Kaminski, and Richard S. Vacca

In the following viewpoint William C. Bosher Jr., Kate R. Kaminski, and Richard S. Vacca argue that advertising in schools benefits students. While the authors acknowledge that corporate involvement with schools has potential drawbacks, they maintain that commercialism in schools can help cash-strapped school districts obtain valuable funding and supplies. The authors assert, however, that schools considering commercialism to meet their needs must not neglect student interests. Bosher is the dean of education at Virginia Commonwealth University, Kaminski is an attorney who specializes in education law, and Vacca is a senior fellow of the Commonwealth Educational Policy Institute at Virginia Commonwealth University.

As you read, consider the following questions:
1. According to the authors, how does California regulate advertising in schools?
2. In the view of the authors, why are school administrators generally not successful negotiators?

William C. Bosher Jr., Kate R. Kaminski, and Richard S. Vacca, *The School Law Handbook: What Every Leader Needs to Know*. Alexandria, VA: Association for Supervision and Curriculum Development, 2004. Copyright © 2004 by the Association for Supervision and Curriculum Development. The Association for Supervision and Curriculum Development is a worldwide community of educators advocating sound policies and sharing best practices to achieve the success of each learner. To learn more, visit ASCD at www.ascd.org. All rights reserved. Reproduced by permission.

In response to consistent student population growth in the district, [a] school board decides to pursue a bond issue to renovate older buildings and to add classroom space. The initiative includes the construction of a new middle school that will house grades 6, 7, and 8. There is much excitement surrounding the construction of the building, which will bring with it enriched educational programs, carefully selected faculty, and fresh leadership.

Widespread Interest from Businesses

The school community, faculty, and students aren't the only ones who are excited; owners of both large and small companies in the district are looking forward to the economic growth the school and its attendant programs will create in the business community. Electrical contractors, plumbers, carpenters, brick layers, architects, and engineers will all have additional work, and the need for materials, technology, and promotional activities for students and parent groups will present a wealth of business opportunities. Perhaps most important to the purveyors of commercial products and services, however, is the powerful market the school will supply—a captive audience of young people.

The new principal, Jim Baxter, is given a year to work on planning and preparation prior to the opening of the school. He spends most of that time selecting faculty and organizing programs, but he also has to deal with a constant stream of vendors proposing "opportunities" and "partnerships." Like most leaders in the public sector, Jim is confronted daily with people far more skilled at selling than he is at buying. Not everyone who visits Jim is selling something, however. Many want to "give" the school a product or service under the auspices of community patronage. A local dentist, for example, wants to give every student a toothbrush with his name on it. Similarly, a pediatrician wants to distribute guidelines for good hygiene along with information about his practice. Retail merchants have book covers and mouse pads featuring the names and logos of their sponsors; fast food restaurants want to give away gadgets and coupons; and a host of businesses—video stores, record shops, shoe outlets—are proffering a plethora of "gifts" for the students, simply in order to gain a market advantage.

A computer company makes a particularly intriguing offer. Each teacher will receive a computer and a lab will be established for students if Jim agrees to endorse the company. Such an endorsement would require Jim to encourage parents and students to purchase their computers from this particular store if they want to be compatible with the software and technology students will be using at school.

Legal and Policy Considerations

Increasingly, schools struggle to retain funding for education. Even as government education budgets shrink, school demands continue to grow, thanks in part to increased accountability. As a result, schools have had to find creative ways to fund their goals. One method of raising additional money or acquiring needed supplies for students is through some form of commercialism. The degree of commercialism varies and may include exclusive contracts, vending relationships, fund raising, naming rights, direct and indirect advertising, sponsorships, endorsements, or leasing school property. Although such opportunities provide much needed cash for schools, they also raise a host of serious legal and policy concerns. According to one survey based on media references, commercialism in schools has been on the rise from 1990 through 2000, with a slight decline, overall, in 2001.

Generally, the legal issues associated with this emerging area fall under contract law and procurement law. Of the two, procurement laws more frequently address commercialism in schools, but by and large, decisions related to this issue have been left to the discretion of school boards. As commercialism in schools becomes more prevalent, however, responses from the public and, hence, legislators are expected. In some states, legislation already addresses commercialism by permitting it, regulating it, or prohibiting some forms of it and allowing others.

Commercialism in schools can provide great advantages for students, staff, parents, and the public, as well as financial relief for government funding sources. The trade off for the extra funding and/or supplies and equipment, however, is students' exposure to advertising, either directly or indirectly, while under compulsory attendance. Corporate America "pays" schools to gain access to students—a profitable market. Although a corporation's goal may be genuinely altruistic, it is always capitalistic as well—namely, to get students and their parents to buy and use certain products and services, and/or to build brand loyalty for future consumers. For example, in the now famous Channel One instance, schools received technology equipment in exchange for student exposure to two minutes of commercials.

Several States' Regulations

Taking a step beyond the general coverage of contract and procurement laws, some states do specifically regulate commercialism in schools, at least in part. According to a recent Government Accounting Office (2000) report, "state laws and regulations governing commercial activities in public schools are not comprehensive and that, in most states, local school officials are responsible for making decisions about commercial activities in public schools." Nonetheless, some state laws do specifically prohibit, restrict, or permit some or all forms of commercialism in schools. The following are examples of such laws and regulations:

N.Y. State Regents Rules § 23.2 prohibits certain promotional activity in schools. "Boards of education or their agents shall not enter into written or oral contracts . . . for which the consideration . . . consists of a promise to permit commercial promotional activity on school premises. . . ."

Wisconsin Code § 118.12(1) allows any person to "sell or promote the sale of goods or services" on school property except as prohibited, restricted, or provided for in school board guidelines.

New Mexico Code § 22-28-1. "The right to sell advertising space on school buses shall be within the sole discretion of the local school board. . . ."

Wisconsin Code § 118.12(4). "If a local school board grants exclusive rights to a soft drink vendor, then "the contract may not prohibit the sale of milk in any school and, to the maximum extent possible, the school board shall ensure that milk is available to pupils in each school covered by the [exclusive] contract."

Florida Code § 1001.43 (2a) and (5). The district school board may adopt policies for (1) "sales calls and demonstra-

Examples of Advertising in Schools

Direct advertising

Advertising in schools, in school facilities, and on school buses:

- Billboards and signs in school corridors, sports facilities, or buses
- Product displays
- Corporate logos or brand names on school equipment, such as marquees, message boards, scoreboards, and backboards
- Ads, corporate logos, or brand names on posters, book covers, and student assignment books

Advertisements in school publications:

- Ads in sports programs, yearbooks, school newspapers, and school calendars . . .

Indirect advertising

Corporate-sponsored educational materials:

- Dental hygiene units that provide toothpaste and toothbrush samples and display brand names
- Materials on issues associated with particular industries that are developed by those industries, such as ecology units produced by oil and plastic companies and safety units produced by insurance companies
- Materials that promote industrial goals, such as energy conservation materials produced by power companies and nutritional information produced by dairy or meat associations

General Accounting Office, *Commercial Activities in Schools*, September 2000.

---

tions by agents, solicitors, sales persons and vendors on campus . . . and (2) advertising in schools for business/community partnerships . . . [and] public solicitations in schools, including the distribution and posting of promotional materials and literature."

California Code § 35182.5. The local school board may not "enter into a contract that grants exclusive advertising or grants the right to the exclusive sale of carbonated beverages . . . unless the [school board] has adopted a policy after a public hearing . . . to ensure that the district has internal controls in place to protect the integrity of the public funds and to ensure that the funds raised benefit public education, and that the contracts are entered into on a competitive basis pursuant to . . . Public Contract Code . . ." or a request for proposals.

The school purchase of goods and services is governed by state and, sometimes, local procurement laws. Depending on the type of commercialism and the value of the potential contract, procurement laws and local procedures may be invoked. It is very important to check state procurement laws and local policies and procedures before entering into any type of commercialism agreement or situation. A request for proposals or even a formal bidding process may be necessary.

Although no federal law regarding commercialism per se exists, national advocacy groups continue to lobby for such. For example, Commercial Alert, a nonprofit organization, is lobbying Congress to pass a "Parents Bill of Rights" that includes a prohibition against advertising in schools. (See http://www.Commercialalert.org for more information.)

Seattle's Rejection of Commercialism

School boards and administrators face pressure both from those who oppose commercialism and those who want additional funds to meet educational goals. Recently, some school boards have responded to this pressure by taking a no commercialism stance. For example, the Seattle School Board decided to phase out Channel One broadcasts. The situation with Channel One was that schools were offered television sets for every classroom in exchange for a block of daily time that students would be permitted to watch "news" and commercials. The deal was a marketing success, with advertisers of everything from jeans to records paying top dollar to get their wares in front of teen buyers. Although many school districts took the deal, others were skeptical of selling to a captive audience assembled through compulsory attendance laws. The Seattle School Board also prohibits advertising on score boards and school buildings, but it does allow logos for identification (rather than advertising). Other boards swing in the opposite direction, advocating commercialism to the fullest extent to provide for cash-strapped schools. Regardless of one's ideological stance on the issue of commercialism, below is a list of suggestions:

Keep student interests at the forefront. Students' attendance at school is compulsory. Should policymakers allow marketers access to this captive audience? Or, are the extra funds so necessary to achieve the school's goals that exposure to marketing is acceptable? Each school board and administrator must make these tough policy choices. Perhaps a certain level of commercialism is acceptable for the cafeteria, but unacceptable for computers or textbooks. The pros and cons of each potential "commercial" contract must be balanced against what is best for students. (In one instance, students were being encouraged to drink soda, even during class, in order to meet the vendor's quota requirements for the maximum pecuniary benefit to the schools.) Health issues, the role of commercialism in schools, and the financial and pedagogical effects of such commercialism must all be considered.

Negotiate legal and practical obstacles with experience. Educators who engage in commercialism frequently express concerns about negotiating with experienced vendors. Administrators may be excellent educators and leaders, but are not usually experienced sellers or buyers as well. Knowing the ins and outs of the contracts and what exactly must be accomplished to receive the maximum financial or product gain is critical. Use knowledgeable and experienced people for negotiating these contracts.

Check state law and local policy.

Develop collective expectations (via staff, school board, community, corporate, and parent input) for school business partnerships. [Lamar Alexander and Richard W. Riley cite] one principal [who] suggests, "Get every corporate . . . partner to engage in a dialogue with students . . . tap [corporate] resources to drive and improve . . . curricula, and bring [the partner] full force into [the education] world at the same time [schools] venture into [the corporate world]."

Weighing the Costs of Commercialism

[Principal] Jim [Baxter] has quickly discovered that in some instances, accepting a "gift" carries too high a price. If the computer company's proposal is consistent with school board policy, he can accept the computers being offered, but if the cost to students, parents, and the community is too great, then he will have to decline.

If no district policy exists that speaks to this request, Jim will need to ask if there are any state laws prohibiting sole source purchasing without extraordinary justification. Have other vendors in the community been given the same opportunity, and would any of them be willing to offer a better proposal? A final caution should rest with the community. Will parents feel comfortable being locked into purchasing from one company? Jim has found that he must be savvy about those who come bearing gifts, and he has realized that true giving does not include an expectation of reciprocation.

"[From 2001 to 2002] youth exposure and overexposure to televised alcohol advertising . . . grew."

Adolescents Are Overexposed to Alcohol Advertising

Center on Alcohol Marketing and Youth

Teenagers are seeing more commercials for alcoholic beverages each year, the Center on Alcohol Marketing and Youth (CAMY) maintains in the following viewpoint. According to the center, adolescent viewing of certain television programs and cable channels makes it more likely that they, and not adults, will be exposed to alcohol commercials. The center asserts that the alcohol industry has not done enough to reduce youth exposure to their ads and contends that more alcohol advertising needs to be shifted away from youth-oriented programming. CAMY, an organization based at Georgetown University, monitors the marketing efforts of the alcohol industry and aims to reduce the appeal of alcohol to minors.

As you read, consider the following questions:

1. According to the center, 90 percent of Americans ages twelve to twenty viewed how many alcohol commercials in 2002?
2. In 2001, of the fifteen television shows most popular with teens, how many aired alcohol advertising, as stated by the center?
3. As explained by the author, why did television advertising for alcohol increase between 2001 and 2002?

Center on Alcohol Marketing and Youth, *Youth Exposure to Alcohol Ads on Television, 2002: From 2001 to 2002, Alcohol's Adland Grew Vaster*, April 21, 2004. Copyright © 2004 by the Center on Alcohol Marketing and Youth. Reproduced by permission.

Unlike magazines or radio, much of television programming reaches a very broad audience demographically. Limiting youth exposure to alcohol advertising on television is thus a more difficult task. Much of youth exposure to alcohol advertising on television comes as a byproduct of exposure to adults, even though youth are not exposed at a higher *rate* per capita than adults to the majority of televised alcohol ads. In fact, youth 12–20 were on average just 10% of the total audience for television shows with alcohol advertising. Nevertheless, a large amount of youth exposure can still result. A good example of this occurs with sports programming. The alcohol industry spent 60% of its television advertising dollars on sports programming, where the average youth audience composition was a mere 8.5%. This is not to say that young people were not exposed to large amounts of alcohol advertising on television. In fact, 90% of youth 12–20 saw on average more than 280 alcohol ads in 2002, 50% saw an average of 507 ads, and the heaviest TV-watching 32% saw an average of 780 ads.

The Whys and Wheres of Overexposure

Youth overexposure to alcohol advertising occurs when youth are over-represented in the audience viewing an alcohol ad, relative to their presence in the general population, and are thus more likely per capita than adults to see the ad. Youth 12–20 are 13.3% of the overall U.S. population [aged] two and above. Only two program categories in 2002 had youth (12–20) audience compositions greater than 13.3%: music video and entertainment, and variety. Not surprisingly, youth saw more ads than adults 21 and above per capita if they were watching these two programming genres: 50% and 29% more, respectively.

Youth were also more likely than adults on a per capita basis to see alcohol advertising on three cable networks: Comedy Central, VH-1 and BET. Alcohol advertisers have suggested in the past that the actual demographic target for their advertising is not the entire legal-age population, but rather young adults 21–34. On two of these outlets—Comedy Central and BET—youth 12–20 were more likely per capita to see the alcohol advertising than young adults 21–34 as well.

Overall on television in 2002, youth 12–20 were more likely than adults on a per capita basis to have seen 66,218 ads, a 30% increase over 2001. This occurred because the proportion of youth in the viewing audience for these advertisements was greater than the presence of youth in the population. These ads were purchased at a cost to the industry of more than $118 million. The ratio of youth overexposure within this subset of television advertising for alcohol was higher than in the equivalent subset in 2001, reflecting a year-to-year increase in every category. For instance, beer ads overexposing youth delivered 73% more exposure to youth than adults in 2001, and 82% more exposure in 2002. Youth not only had significantly greater exposure to the 66,218 ads that overexposed them in 2002 than adults 21 and above, but also were more likely on a per capita basis to have seen them than young adults 21–34. Beer and low-alcohol refresher marketers placed the majority of overexposing ads.

Indeed, the 20 brands spending the most money to place advertising that overexposed youth were dominated by beers and low-alcohol refreshers. Most of these brands were among the highest spending alcohol advertisers on television. Taken together, they accounted for nearly 80% of the spending on alcohol advertising overexposing youth. For some of these brands, expenditures on overexposing ads accounted for more than a quarter of the brand's total expenditures, and for most of them, more than a quarter of the brand's total ads.

Advertising on Popular Shows

Another measure of youth exposure to alcohol advertising on television can be gained by looking at advertising on the programs most popular with teens 12–17 in a typical week of the 2002 television season. As in CAMY's report on alcohol advertising on television in 2001 [*Television: Alcohol's Vast Adland*], this analysis selected a week comparable to the time period used by the Federal Trade Commission (FTC) in its 1999 report on self-regulation in the alcohol industry. During one week in October of 1998, the FTC found alcohol advertising on at least three of the 15 programs most popular with teens aged 12–17. In 2001, CAMY found advertising on 13 of the 15 programs most popular with teens.

In 2002, all of the programs most popular with teens 12–17 during the week of October 14–20 had alcohol advertising during the 2002 calendar year. Throughout that year, alcohol companies placed 5,085 ads on these programs, at a total cost of nearly $53 million. Spending on this group of shows increased by 60% compared with 2001. Six of the shows—five on WB, one on Fox—had disproportionately youthful audiences (that is, their youth audience compositions exceeded 13.3%. . .).

Top 10 Teen Television Programs (Week of 10/14/02 to 10/20/02) and Alcohol Ads in 2002

Rank	Net-work	Program	Ads	Dollars	Network/ Spot	Youth 12–20 Audience >13.3%
1	CBS	*CSI*	312	$2,484,662	Spot, Network	N
2	NBC	*Friends*	615	$17,682,999	Spot, Network	N
3	CBS	*Survivor: Thailand*	124	$1,904,160	Spot, Network	N
4	WB	*Smallville*	387	$745,761	Spot	Y
5	NBC	*E.R.*	364	$5,812,726	Spot, Network	N
6	NBC	*Fear Factor*	1,088	$7,196,669	Spot, Network	N
7	WB	*7th Heaven*	12	$7,042	Spot	Y
8	NBC	*Scrubs*	312	$3,652,616	Spot, Network	N
9	NBC	*Will & Grace*	463	$10,090,876	Spot, Network	N
10	WB	*Angel*	125	$115,438	Spot	Y

Center on Alcohol Marketing and Youth, 2002.

The alcohol industry's principal method of limiting youth exposure to its advertising is through voluntary codes of good marketing practice. These codes are published by the three leading trade associations: the Beer Institute, the Distilled Spirits Council of the United States (DISCUS), and the Wine Institute. Individual companies may also adopt their own voluntary codes. In September 2003, the Beer Institute and DIS-CUS announced revisions of their voluntary codes, lowering the maximum youth audience composition for their advertising from 50% to 30%, matching the 30% standard the Wine Institute Code had set in December 2000.

Examination of alcohol advertising on television in 2002 reveals that this change is a step in the right direction. A threshold setting youth 12–20 audience composition at a maximum of 30% in 2002 would have required alcohol marketers to move or eliminate 12% of their advertisements, representing 5% of spending and 22% of youth alcohol advertising impressions.

However, it would still have permitted substantial youth overexposure to alcohol advertising on television. The National Research Council and the Institute of Medicine (IOM), in a recent report to Congress on how best to reduce underage drinking, recommended that the alcohol industry immediately adopt a standard barring alcohol advertising on programs where youth 12–20 are more than 25% of the total audience, as a first step toward eventual adoption of a more proportional threshold of 15%. The latter threshold would make substantially more difference in reducing the exposure of underage youth to alcohol advertising on television. If the industry had adhered to a 15% threshold in 2002, 61,741 ads—more than one in five alcohol ads on television —would have had to have been moved to less youth-oriented programming or pulled, affecting 40% of youth alcohol advertising impressions. Shifting or removing this advertising would have gone a long way toward eliminating the 66,218 alcohol ads that youth 12–20 were more likely than adults 21+ to view on television in 2002.

Setting Stricter Standards

Television advertising for alcohol increased from 2001 to 2002. This increase resulted at least in part from two trends within the alcohol industry: the growth of low-alcohol refreshers as a beverage category and the increasing presence of distilled spirits advertising on television. Youth exposure and overexposure to televised alcohol advertising also grew. In 2002, youth ages 12–20 saw two beer and distilled spirits ads on television for every three seen by adults, and nearly three advertisements for low-alcohol refreshers for every four seen by adults. Youth saw more than two television advertisements for beer and ale for every three ads for carbonated soft drinks, a product more normally associated with youth.

Despite the recent tightening of their voluntary marketing codes by brewers and distillers, the analysis in this report suggests that, if it had been in effect in 2002, even the stricter standard of 30% maximum youth audience composition would have permitted substantial youth overexposure to alcohol advertising on television.

This [viewpoint] provides further support for the recommendation by the IOM that alcohol companies adopt a standard for youth audience composition that is closer to the actual proportion of youth 12–20 in the general population. Nielsen measures television audiences beginning at age two. Youth 12–20, the population tracked by federal surveys measuring underage drinking, are less than 14% of the general population two and above. The Institute of Medicine's recommended threshold of 15% maximum youth audience composition for alcohol advertising would leave 77% of television programming still accessible to alcohol advertising since only 23% of the programs monitored by Nielsen on television in 2002 had youth (12–20) audience compositions greater than 15%. Yet in 2002, a 15% threshold would have affected 40% of youth exposure to alcohol advertising.

The IOM's recommendation is sensible and reasonable and should be adopted by alcohol companies in order to stem the growing tide of youth exposure to alcohol advertising on television.

"Even if the evidence that ads encourage underage drinking were stronger, brewers . . . would still have a First Amendment right to communicate with their customers."

Alcohol Advertising Does Not Target Children

Jacob Sullum

Television commercials for alcoholic beverages are not aimed at underage viewers, Jacob Sullum claims in the following viewpoint. Sullum criticizes a report that accuses the alcohol industry of airing commercials on programs popular among teenagers and thereby encouraging underage drinking. According to Sullum, alcohol advertisers cannot avoid exposing a young audience because they advertise on many of the shows that appeal to teenagers as well as to young adults. He further contends that even if teenagers are exposed to a significant number of advertisements for alcoholic beverages, there is no evidence that these commercials encourage underage drinking. Sullum is a senior editor at *Reason* magazine.

As you read, consider the following questions:

1. According to Sullum, which shows from the list provided by the Center on Alcohol Marketing and Youth (CAMY) had the fewest alcohol advertisements?
2. According to the author, how does CAMY misinterpret a statement by the Federal Trade Commission?
3. In Sullum's view, what accompanies a positive attitude toward drinking?

"**O**ne quarter of alcohol advertising on television in 2001 was more likely to be seen by youth than adults," Georgetown University's Center on Alcohol Marketing and Youth (CAMY) announced [in December 2002]. Not only that, but "youth saw more commercials for beer than for juice, gum, chips, sneakers or jeans."

If your blood is not already boiling at the very thought of "youth" being "exposed" to ads for Budweiser and Mike's Hard Lemonade, you should have a look at CAMY's 20-page report, "Television: Alcohol's Vast Adland." It will outrage anyone who values intellectual honesty.

Banal Accusations

CAMY's main overt accusation is that manufacturers of alcoholic beverages are recklessly exposing "underage youths" (i.e., 12-to-20-year-olds) to ads that make drinking look fun. The report uses impressive-sounding figures to insinuate that the industry deliberately targets underage drinkers. But CAMY's calculations dissolve into banality upon close examination.

"In calendar year 2001," CAMY reports, "the alcohol industry . . . placed 1,441 ads on 13 of the 15 prime time network programs with the largest teen audiences." Those shows included *Survivor, Friends, E.R., CSI, That '70s Show*, and *Buffy the Vampire Slayer*—all of which are popular with adults as well as minors. The shows on the list that seem to skew most toward teenagers are also the ones that attracted the fewest alcohol ads: *7th Heaven*, for example, had five, while *Gilmore Girls* had six, compared to 429 for *Friends* and 382 for *That '70s Show*.

CAMY even complains about alcoholic beverage commercials on *Saturday Night Live*. Advertisers cannot reach large numbers of adult viewers, especially the young adults prized by beer and "malternative" producers, without also reaching large numbers of viewers who are not old enough to drink legally. How many shows on TV appeal to 21-year-olds but not to 20-year-olds? Combine the impossibility of making such fine distinctions with the fact that 12-to-20-year-olds watch a lot of TV, and it's not exactly surprising that they see a lot of alcohol ads: 245 on average in 2001, according to CAMY. But so what?

CAMY claims "research clearly indicates that, in addition to parents and peers, alcohol advertising and marketing have a significant impact on youth decisions to drink." The first clue that the research does not clearly indicate this comes in the Federal Trade Commission statement that CAMY quotes: "While many factors may influence an underage person's drinking decisions, including among other things parents, peers and media, there is reason to believe that advertising also plays a role." Notice how CAMY has upgraded "a role" into "a significant impact" and transformed a hypothesis "there is reason to believe" into a fact that "research clearly indicates."

Companies Are Responding

In the last 10 years, the beverage alcohol industry has responded voluntarily to FTC staff investigations with changes to its codes. . . . Examples of voluntary industry responses to problematic practices include:

• Withdrawing ads from television programs with majority underage audiences: In the mid-1990's, FTC staff investigated the placement of beer ads on cable network programming that had majority underage audiences. The companies withdrew the ads from the programming at issue, and the Beer Institute adopted the requirement that demographic data be reviewed periodically to reduce the likelihood that the problem would recur.

• Applying code protections to Internet ads: In 1997, FTC staff reviewed alcohol web sites, which some industry observers believed were potentially attractive to minors. At the time, it was unclear whether web sites were covered by the industry advertising codes. Responding to these concerns, the Beer Institute and DISCUS [Distilled Spirits Council of the United States] modified their codes to clarify that they applied to advertising online.

Federal Trade Commission, "A Review of Industry Efforts to Avoid Promoting Alcohol to Underage Consumers," September 1999.

The reason for the FTC's cautious language is clear from the quality of the evidence CAMY offers to prove that ads make teenagers drink. It cites a couple of studies that found kids who recalled and liked alcohol ads more were more likely to drink or express an intention to do so. All such research shows is that a positive attitude toward drinking goes along with an affection for beer commercials. It does not show that the commercials cause the attitude.

The rest of CAMY's evidence is even lamer: kids' familiarity with the Budweiser frogs, surveys in which people express the opinion that ads make drinking more appealing, a statement by the National Association of Broadcasters that "radio and television audiences, particularly kids," like "clever jingles, flashy lights, fast talking, and quick pacing." The sad thing is that you have to assume CAMY is making the strongest case it can. It doesn't help that underage drinking has been declining in recent years. It's hard to whip up hysteria about a shrinking problem.

Even if the evidence that ads encourage underage drinking were stronger, brewers, vintners, and distillers would still have a First Amendment right to communicate with their customers. "No one is policing what the industry is doing," complains CAMY adviser David A. Kessler, former Commissioner of the Food and Drug Administration. Yet CAMY Executive Director Mike O'Hara, who used to work for Kessler at the FDA, says the organization is not calling for censorship—not right now, at least.

"We feel the first thing is to get the data out," O'Hara told the *New York Times*, "and then have a vigorous public policy debate about what are the appropriate public health protections for our youth." It's always good to have a vigorous debate before you force your opponents to shut up.

Periodical Bibliography

The following articles have been selected to supplement the diverse views presented in this chapter.

Andrea Bell	"Putting Kids Before Commercialism," *Education Digest*, May 2002.
Kim Campbell and Kent Davis-Packard	"How Ads Get Kids to Say, 'I Want It!'" *Christian Science Monitor*, September 18, 2000.
Edward Cohn	"Consuming Kids," *American Prospect*, January 31, 2000.
Martin Glenn, Craig Smith, and Debra Shipley	"The Kids Question," *Marketing*, February 12, 2004.
Katy Kelly and Linda Kulman	"Kid Power," *U.S. News & World Report*, September 13, 2004.
Ellen Neuborne	"For Kids on the Web, It's an Ad, Ad, Ad, Ad World," *BusinessWeek Online*, August 13, 2001.
Kimberly Pohlman	"The Commercialization of Children's Television," *Extra!* May/June 2000.
Nina Riccio	"How Alcohol Ads Target Teens," *Current Health 2*, September 2002.
Jonathan Rowe	"The Parents' Bill of Rights," *Mothering*, January/February 2003.
Juliet Schor, interviewed by Andrea Sachs	"Junk Culture," *Time*, October 4, 2004.
Michael Snider	"Hey Kids! Let's Play Adver-Games!" *Maclean's*, December 23, 2002.
Mary Story and Simone French	"Food Advertising and Marketing Directed at Children and Adolescents in the U.S.," *International Journal of Behavioral Nutrition and Physical Activity*, February 10, 2004.

CHAPTER 3

Should Political Advertising Be Reformed?

Chapter Preface

The 2004 presidential election featured some of the most negative political commercials in American history. One advertisement questioned Senator John Kerry's actions in the Vietnam War, claiming that he was not the war hero he purported to be. Meanwhile, opponents of President George W. Bush ran commercials castigating his economic policies and his decision to go to war in Iraq in 2003. These and other negative commercials have led many people to believe that American politics have never been uglier. However, mudslinging has long been a part of presidential election campaigns. Experts point out that television may make it easier for political parties and their supporters to spread negative propaganda, but otherwise little has changed in more than two centuries.

As *Detroit Free Press* political writer Chris Bell points out, "Character assassination is the occasional by-product of open, competitive politics, and is as American as apple pie." Several eighteenth- and nineteenth-century campaigns were especially nasty. In the 1800 election the campaigns for John Adams and Thomas Jefferson let loose with invective that would shock many Americans today. Jefferson supporters described Adams as being old, blind, and toothless, and accused him of keeping mistresses and desiring to establish an American monarchy. Adams's advocates labeled Jefferson a Francophile, who must be kept from the presidency lest he bring with him the practices of murder, adultery, and incest.

The 1860 election featured campaign literature that made fun of Abraham Lincoln's appearance and ran cartoons with racist overtones, such as those depicting Lincoln as a monkey. In a nation divided over slavery, such racist politicking could be effective, although it did not prevent Lincoln's election. The 1876 campaign between James Blaine and Grover Cleveland led to one of the most negative political slogans in American history: "Ma, ma, where's my pa? Gone to the White House, ha-ha-ha." The slogan referred to the bachelor Cleveland's relationship with Maria Halpin, who had given birth to a son. Although the boy's parentage could not be proved, as Cleveland was not Halpin's only lover, he paid child support until the boy was adopted. Americans that year ignored the negative campaigning and elected Cleveland.

The invention of television has both helped and hindered negative campaigning. Television makes it easier for political parties and organizations to spread falsehoods or raise questions about the opponents' character and how he would act as president. Among the more memorable television commercials was the Lyndon B. Johnson campaign's "daisy" advertisement of 1964, which suggested that Republican candidate Barry Goldwater would lead America into nuclear war. Also notable was the Willie Horton commercial that aired during the 1988 campaign between George H.W. Bush and Michael Dukakis; the ad left viewers wondering if the latter candidate would be tough on crime. However, candidates who are attacked also can use television to immediately refute the contents of negative advertisements; they or their representatives can appear on one of several twenty-four-hour news channels right after the commercial first airs.

Negative campaigning may not be new to American politics but that does not mean it has to remain part of every election. The authors in the following chapter debate whether political advertising needs to be reformed. With more than two centuries of mudslinging, it may be difficult for American politicians to adopt a new approach, but many analysts believe it is worth exploring the possibilities.

"[In 2004] more ads than ever focused on discrediting an opponent rather than promoting a candidate."

Political Advertising Is Becoming Increasingly Negative

Janet Hook

According to Janet Hook in the following viewpoint, while negative campaigning has long been a part of American politics, such invective has been on the rise over the past two decades. She argues that politicians and political organizations are relying on tactics such as linking the opposing candidate to terrorism and questioning his or her integrity. According to Hook, negative political advertising discourages many qualified community leaders from running for public office. Hook is a staff writer for the *Los Angeles Times*.

As you read, consider the following questions:

1. What has been the "dubious hallmark" of the 2004 election, in the author's opinion?
2. Why was Tom Daschle targeted by the Family Research Council, according to the author?
3. According to Hook, what is one possible consequence of negative campaigning on governance?

[In 2001] a line was quietly crossed in the annals of political history.

In newspapers across South Dakota, an out-of-state conservative group ran a political ad linking a Democratic senator to former Iraqi President Saddam Hussein. Critics cried foul, saying it breached standards of political decency.

That was then. This is now, and campaign efforts to link politicians to terrorists are a dime a dozen. And they are coming not from little-known fringe groups but from such pillars of the political establishment as the Speaker of the House.

Therein lies the dubious hallmark of the 2004 election cycle. It has evolved into one of the most relentlessly negative political campaigns in memory, as attacks on a candidate's character, patriotism and fitness for office, which once seemed out of bounds, have become routine. More ads than ever focused on discrediting an opponent rather than promoting a candidate, independent analysts said. And, the analysts warned, the presidential campaign was breaking new ground in a candidate's willingness to bend the truth.

"There is a very high level of factual inaccuracy out there," said Kathleen Hall Jamieson, director of the University of Pennsylvania's Annenberg Public Policy Center, whose website, http://www.factcheck.org, has identified dozens of major distortions in presidential campaign ads and speeches [in 2004]. . . .

A History of Negativity

The 2004 campaign has become the kind of race that would warm the heart of Lee Atwater, the architect of the successful 1988 presidential race by [George W.] Bush's father. The GOP'S hard-hitting attacks on Democrat Michael S. Dukakis that year were viewed as a watershed in the escalation of negative campaigning. One of Atwater's sidekicks in the campaign was none other than the candidate's son—George W. Bush.

Of course, Atwater did not invent negative campaigning. The 1800 presidential campaign was an early example of an especially nasty one. John Adams was accused of being a monarchist. His rival, Thomas Jefferson, was accused of being a French sympathizer at a time when foreign entanglements were viewed with particular alarm.

But negative campaigning acquired new intensity and broader reach when technology transferred it from partisan pamphlets to television ads. An early example of the emotional wallop a TV ad could carry came in 1964, when President Lyndon B. Johnson contrasted the images of a little girl counting flower petals with a mushroom cloud to suggest that electing Republican Barry Goldwater would increase the risk of nuclear war.

Some were reminded of that ad when Republicans alleged [in 2004] that [John] Kerry's election would make a terrorist attack more likely. But two differences are striking. The anti-Goldwater ad was so shocking to its audience that it was pulled after only one airing. And the ad itself was nuanced compared to the frontal assaults of today: In 1964, Goldwater's name was not mentioned; in 2004, Bush and Vice President Dick Cheney themselves have implied that the world would be a more dangerous place if Kerry were elected.

The Terrorism Tactic

During the 2002 midterm campaign, when images of terrorists were first deployed to discredit the opposition, it was a controversial tactic that drew national attention. One of the first was the 2001 ad in South Dakota by the conservative Family Research Council, which ran pictures of [then-Senator Tom] Daschle and Saddam Hussein and accused the senator of helping keep Hussein in power. Daschle was not even on the ballot in 2002; he was under attack because, as the leader of senate Democrats, he was seen by conservatives as an obstacle to the Bush administration's agenda in Congress. Later, another conservative group sent a mailing that compared Daschle to Taliban sympathizer John Walker Lindh.

Now, the specter of terrorism is routinely invoked in ads and campaign rhetoric that often cast aspersions on a candidate's patriotism. Bush ads have used terrorist images to paint Kerry as a weak leader. House Speaker J. Dennis Hastert (R-Ill.) took it a step further when he said Al Qaeda [terrorist] leaders probably wanted Kerry to win the election. A Democratic National Committee ad, meanwhile, has accused Bush of flagging in the hunt for [terrorist Osama] Bin Laden.

"It's always tempting to say the campaign you're in is the worst ever, but this time it might actually be true," said Kenneth M. Goldstein, director of the University of Wisconsin Advertising Project.

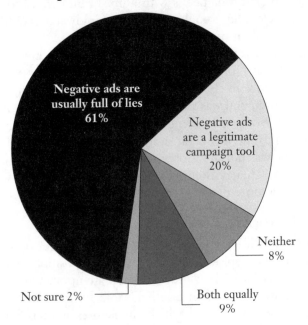

Public Opinion on Negative Campaign Ads

Negative ads are usually full of lies 61%

Negative ads are a legitimate campaign tool 20%

Neither 8%

Not sure 2%

Both equally 9%

Issues and Controversies On File, April 9, 2004.

This year, he added, there is "something that's qualitatively different: You always had wacky things said by fringe groups. Now you're seeing it by mainstream groups and the candidates themselves."...

Debating the Effectiveness

The profusion of divisive, ill-founded rhetoric has been abetted by changes in technology and the media since the last campaign. The explosion of communication on the Internet has vastly increased the opportunities for attacks through a medium that seems to prize speed over accuracy. Additionally, cut-and-thrust arguments play well to the faster-paced, more partisan cable news shows that have multiplied in recent years.

The politics of attack have also flourished because of a consensus among politicians and their consultants that "going negative" is effective.

"The public may say they don't like attack ads, but they do work," said Tony Coelho, a former Democratic congressman from Merced [California] and party insider.

"Once you raise a question about somebody, if there's an ounce of credibility, it sticks. It's easier to believe negative things than positive things."

But [professor of communications William] Benoit argued that voters' reactions to negative campaigning depended on what kind of attack is being launched. His study of presidential campaign messages from 1948 to 2000 found that the candidates who attacked on policy grounds were more likely to be winners; those who attacked on character were more likely to be losers.

The politics of 2004—on the campaign trail and off—is not just negative and sometimes misleading; it also has a coarse, personal edge. Bush and Kerry attacked not just each other's positions on issues, but each other's personal credibility and integrity. In the Oklahoma Senate race, [Tom] Coburn has called his contest against Democratic Rep. Brad Carson a "battle between good and evil." When Cheney met a Democratic critic on the Senate floor earlier this year, he responded with an obscenity rarely heard in public dialogue. In campaigns around the country, opponents are not just criticized; they are demonized.

A More Polarized Electorate

Some analysts see this trend stemming from a major change in the political agenda: the emergence of more social issues with a moral dimension. Such issues as abortion, school prayer and gay marriage are more likely to provoke polarized, unbridgeable disagreements than the economic and foreign policy issues that dominated in the past.

"It's one thing to say someone is wrong; it's another to say someone is immoral," said William A. Galston, a former advisor to President [Bill] Clinton. "I think there once was more of a sense that politics was a competition among well-intentioned and patriotic leaders with different visions of what would serve the national interest."

Some argued that the preponderance of negative campaigning and the polarization of politics had a positive aspect—it is a powerful way to clarify contrasts between two candidates or the two major parties.

Nor does [2004's] harsh tone seem to be turning off voters. Indeed, given reports of big increases in voter registration, it may be fueling—not dampening—passion and interest in the campaign.

Discouraging Political Involvement

Still, many analysts worried about the long-term effects of the increasingly fierce quality of political discourse. They feared that with both Bush and Kerry claiming they wanted to tackle a backlog of problems that would require bipartisan solutions—curbing the federal budget deficit, shoring up Social Security and controlling healthcare costs—the political climate would hamper whoever was elected.

"At the end of this, you are going to have a president hobbled," said Eric M. Uslaner, a political scientist at the University of Maryland. "It's going to be impossible for anyone to govern once this campaign is over."

The venomous character of political campaigns and congressional debate may have another long-term consequence: driving away from public service people who do not have a stomach for that sort of combat.

Three political scientists in 2002 conducted a survey of potential candidates for the House and found that about 64% of them said that the negativism of campaign politics discouraged them from running for office.

It was not always like this. [James] Leach, the Iowa congressman, said that in the 19th century, the Legislature in his state was packed with community leaders—bankers, successful farmers, prominent educators.

"Today that isn't the case," said Leach. "America has never been better-led in the arts, science and business. But leadership of the American political system is not as strong."

> "If [a candidate] is truly interested in improving society . . . then he must tell on his opponent when he misbehaves."

Negative Political Advertising Is Necessary

David Limbaugh

Negative campaigning can be beneficial if truthful, David Limbaugh asserts in the following viewpoint. He argues that negative political commercials help inform voters by providing them with needed information on a candidate's character, voting record, and platform. Limbaugh is an attorney and a syndicated columnist.

As you read, consider the following questions:

1. What are participants in a democratic society obligated to do, in Limbaugh's opinion?
2. What type of campaigning does Limbaugh consider unfair?
3. According to the author, what is worse than dirty campaigning?

David Limbaugh, "The Virtues of Going Negative," Worldnetdaily.com, September 8, 2000. Copyright © 2000 by Creators Syndicate. Reproduced by permission.

I'm sorry, but I'm growing a bit weary of all this negative talk about negative campaigning. I think it's time we started being positive about this gloriously negative American tradition.

Who says negative campaigning is negative? Don't you agree that it's a positive force in a democratic society—OK, a "constitutional republic" for you nitpickers? Let's consider the principles involved.

Negative Ads Keep Voters Informed

First, it is generally a good thing for voters to be informed, on the theory that informed voters make better choices. Underlying this premise, though, is the corollary assumption that the candidates should provide reliable information to the voters—being informed with erroneous data obviously is not desirable.

Next, shouldn't we come down off of our collective high horses and squarely face the truth that being informed means knowing about as many facts as possible, negative as well as positive? As participants in a democratic society, we all have an obligation to contribute information to the political discourse. Even if you don't accept that idea, surely you will agree that, at a minimum, the press has that obligation. Wasn't that one of the driving forces behind the First Amendment?

Yes, you say, but how do you combat disinformation? How do you counteract lies? I'm glad you asked because that brings me to the point about being negative, which is a positive. When candidates or their surrogates are disseminating false information either about themselves, their opponents or the issues, they must be exposed. If we keep our eyes on the big ball, we will understand that such negative exposure is a positive. Is it negative campaigning? Yes, but remember: Negative campaigning is not a negative. Negative campaigning is talking negatively about your opponent, his programs, his character, his record or his lies. There's nothing negative in being negative about negatives. In fact, it's a positive step toward properly informing the voters.

It is just plain silly to suggest that there's anything wrong with a candidate going positively negative in this manner. If he is truly interested in improving society—and if he isn't,

122

that's surely, a negative thing—then he must tell on his opponent when he misbehaves, even though tattletales are generally seen in a negative light.

Negativity Versus Lying

We probably would not be obsessing about so-called "negative campaigning" if we were not knee-deep in this regrettable Clintonian[1] age of semantic and linguistic confusion (please excuse the double negative). However, we live at a time when words—through misuse, overuse and abuse—have sometimes lost their meaning.

The word "negative," of course, has a negative connotation. However, in the context of campaigning it shouldn't. Properly defined, negative campaigning is affirmatively positive.

When Negative Ads Are Useful

A negative ad is not good or bad based exclusively on content, nor whether it is funny, entertaining, or well produced. The most important element is how useful the information is judged to be. For instance, conventional wisdom suggests an ad that alludes to the sexual exploits of a married candidate outside of marriage is inappropriate. If the criterion simply was "below the belt," the ad, based on this view, would be rejected and likely produce a backlash. In reality, though, the ad, which the attacker's campaign organization had predicted would have powerful effects, has virtually no impact since the extramarital activities of the attacked candidate were widely known. The information was old news and therefore judged not useful.

Ruth Ann Weaver Lariscy and Spencer F. Tinkham, *USA Today Magazine*, May 2004.

So what should be out of bounds in the world of politics? Is everything fair in this cynical age? No way, not no how. What is not fair is lying about your opponent, his programs, his character or his truths—it is not fair to characterize the truth as a lie. And while we're on this point, let me add that I don't want to hear any nonsense about the relativity of truth. Yes,

---

1. President Bill Clinton was accused of manipulating language to serve his political goals. For example, according to his detractors, he claimed that oral sex was not really sex.

there are gray areas, but facts are facts, and it is not OK to distort the facts. Lying is bereft of positive qualities. We mustn't call these negative practices "negative campaigning" anymore. Carvillian[2] propagandists have seen to it that this phrase no longer has any meaning. The confusion allows them to avert legitimate criticism by accusing their opponents of being negative when they are just trying to inform voters. Henceforth, we must insist that "negative campaigning" has a positive connotation. Instead, let's call those unsavory practices "dirty campaigning."

What's even worse than dirty campaigning is when the media assists a dirty campaigner to do his dirty deeds by establishing moral equivalency between his dirty campaigning and his opponent's mere negative campaigning. That allows the dirty campaigner's dirty campaigning to be seen in a less negative light, and there is nothing positive about that.

2. referring to Democratic pundit James Carville

*"A ban on corporate and labor advertising
in federal elections [is] fully consistent with
high court precedents."*

Campaign-Finance Reform Will Improve Political Advertising

Trevor Potter

In the following viewpoint Trevor Potter maintains that a reform of campaign-finance laws will help clean up political advertising. He argues that banning the use of "soft money" —contributions given to political parties that purportedly cannot be used in federal elections but in fact are utilized to fund political advertisements—will encourage public confidence in the political system. He further maintains that such reforms are constitutional. Potter, former chairman of the Federal Election Commission, is president of and legal counsel for the Campaign Legal Center, a nonpartisan organization that works to ensure that the public interest is represented in the enforcement of campaign-finance and related media laws.

As you read, consider the following questions:

1. According to Potter, when did Congress first ban the use of corporate money in federal elections?
2. What connection does the author draw between voter turnout and campaign-finance laws?
3. Why does Potter believe that the Ney-Wynn bill would not ban soft money contributions?

Trevor Potter, "Time to Restore Trust in Our Campaign System," *The Christian Science Monitor*, July 12, 2001. Copyright © 2001 by *The Christian Science Monitor*. Reproduced by permission of the author.

C ongress passed the last major campaign-finance reform in 1974, in the wake of Watergate. [On July 12, 2001,] the House of Representatives will vote on another reform bill, known as Shays-Meehan.[1]

The current ills may have different names—"soft money," "issue advocacy," selling the Lincoln bedroom—but the complaint is the same as in 1974: Large contributors and their money appear to have too much sway over our government decisionmaking process.

Does this mean reform is hopeless? No, it just means that no law is a permanent fix, and every reform will have to be strengthened over time. After all, Congress banned corporate money in federal elections in 1907. By 1971, no one took the ban seriously, until several CEOs were convicted of secretly contributing corporate money to President [Richard] Nixon's reelection campaign. After that, and the 1974 reforms, no one gave corporate money to federal candidates for years— until soft money (funds given to political parties under the fiction that they won't be used in federal elections) took hold. Now reformers are trying to restore the old prohibitions—no corporate or labor money in federal elections, and no unlimited individual contributions to federal candidates or parties.

The Spread of Soft Money

The reform that passed the Senate [in 2001,] the McCain-Feingold-Cochran bill, banned soft money to national political parties and prohibited state parties from using it in federal elections. It also prohibited corporations and labor unions from using their money to target TV ads about federal candidates in their districts in the days before an election, and requires that others who run such ads disclose their spending.

Both parties have grown used to the virtually unlimited flow of soft money used by the national parties to pay for television ads, consultants, pollsters, buildings, and travel to resorts. So it's no surprise that the people who spend this money—and some who give it—are loath to get off the gravy train.

Some members of Congress go further and claim the system

1. The bill passed and was signed into law in March 2002.

is necessary to finance vital party activities like voter registration and turnout. This is a true distortion of reality. Voter turnout was higher in the mid-'70s and the '80s when contributions were strictly limited. Further, the amount of soft money spent today by the national parties on voter registration and get-out-the-vote-activity is quite small. Let's clean up the system, and boost public confidence. That might really improve turnout!

Campaign-Finance Reform Is Constitutional

Opponents of reform also claim that the principal provisions of the McCain-Feingold/Shays-Meehan bills are unconstitutional. Earlier [in 2001], a letter signed by every one of the Amercian Civil Liberties Union's past presidents and senior officials supported the constitutionality of the Senate bill.

Political Spending in 2004

Following are details of the estimated $3.9 billion spent on the just-ended federal campaigns:

- Individual contributions to candidates and parties: *$2.5 billion*
- [Political Action Committees'] contributions to candidates and parties: *$384 million*
- Candidates' self-funding: *$144 million*
- Section 527* spending (on federal elections): *$386 million*
- Public funding of presidential candidates and party conventions: *$207 million*
- Convention host committee spending: *$139 million*
- Other spending (including loans and independent expenditures): *$102 million*

* "527" political organizations are not regulated by the Federal Election Commission. They deal exclusively with soft money contributions.

Ward Harkavy, *Village Voice*, November 2, 2004.

[In June 2001,] a Supreme Court decision in a Colorado case demonstrated that the court has a clear understanding of the dangers posed by large contributions to political parties from special interests.

No one can predict how the Supreme Court would rule on every provision of a new campaign-finance law. However, the two key parts of reform—banning soft money in federal elections and a ban on corporate and labor advertising in federal elections—are fully consistent with high court precedents of many years' standing. In the *Buckley v. Valeo* case in 1976, the Court upheld the constitutionality of limits on contributions to political parties, because they protect against "the actuality and appearance of corruption."

A Useless Alternative

Finally, House opponents of real campaign-finance reform hope that the public can be fooled into thinking that any bill labelled reform does the trick—without a look at the contents. The House leadership is now supporting the Ney-Wynn bill, which does virtually nothing to limit soft money, but greatly increases the hard money contributions to political parties.

Under Ney, someone could give the six Republican and Democratic national party committees a total of $450,000 per year, and anything above that could be raised without limit by the president or House and Senate leaders for state parties. Those state parties could then spend the money on the same ads featuring federal candidates that they do now. Some soft money ban! Meanwhile, the annual limit on contributions of "hard" (federal) money to the national committees goes from $25,000 a year to $90,000 a year, per person. The Ney bill may be many things, but a compromise reform measure it is not.

"*It's* logically impossible *both to honor the First Amendment and to regulate campaign finance effectively.*"

Campaign-Finance Reform Violates the First Amendment

Robert J. Samuelson

Campaign-finance reform laws are incompatible with the right to free speech, Robert J. Samuelson opines in the following viewpoint. According to Samuelson, by placing limits on federal campaign contributions and by restricting communications between parties and their candidates, these laws wrongfully infringe on candidates' rights to freely air their political views. He further contends that campaign-finance laws will inevitably fail to reinvigorate the public's confidence in America's political system because citizens will recognize that their rights of free speech and political association are being violated. Samuelson is a columnist for the *Washington Post* and a contributing editor at *Newsweek*.

As you read, consider the following questions:

1. What are First Amendment rights governed by, in Samuelson's opinion?
2. According to Samuelson, what absurd rules is the Democratic National Committee obligated to follow?
3. According to the author, what will be the effects if campaign-finance laws are laxly enforced?

The presidential campaign has confirmed that, under the guise of "campaign finance reform," Congress and the Supreme Court have repealed large parts of the First Amendment. They have simply discarded what were once considered constitutional rights of free speech and political association. It is not that these rights have vanished. But they are no longer constitutional guarantees. They're governed by limits and qualifications imposed by Congress, the courts, state legislatures, regulatory agencies—and lawyers' interpretations of all of the above.

We have entered an era of constitutional censorship. Hardly anyone wants to admit this—the legalized demolition of the First Amendment would seem shocking—and so hardly anyone does. The evidence, though, abounds. The latest is the controversy over the anti–[John] Kerry ads by Swift Boat Veterans for Truth and parallel anti–[George W.] Bush ads by Democratic "527" groups[1] such as MoveOn.org. Let's assume (for argument's sake) that everything in these ads is untrue. Still, the United States political tradition is that voters judge the truthfulness and relevance of campaign arguments. We haven't wanted our political speech filtered.

Gutting the First Amendment

Now there's another possibility. The government may screen what voters see and hear. The Kerry campaign has asked the Federal Election Commission (FEC) to ban the Swift Boat ads; the Bush campaign similarly wants the FEC to suppress the pro-Democrat 527 groups. We've arrived at this juncture because it's *logically impossible* both to honor the First Amendment and to regulate campaign finance effectively. We can do one or the other—but not both. Unfortunately, Congress and the Supreme Court won't admit the choice. The result is the worst of both worlds. We gut the First Amendment and don't effectively regulate campaign finance.

The First Amendment says that Congress "shall make no law . . . abridging the freedom of speech, or . . . the right of the people peaceably to assemble, and to petition the Govern-

---

1. These are political organizations that accept unlimited soft money contributions and are not regulated by the Federal Election Commission.

ment" (that's "political association"). The campaign finance laws, the latest being McCain-Feingold,[2] blatantly violate these prohibitions. The Supreme Court has tried to evade the contradiction. It has allowed limits on federal campaign contributions. It justifies the limits as preventing "corruption" or "the appearance of corruption." But the court has rejected limits on overall campaign spending by candidates, parties or groups. Limiting spending, the court says, would violate free speech. Spending enables candidates to reach voters through TV and other media.

Unfortunately, this artful distinction doesn't work. If groups can spend any amount on campaigns, their spending can easily become unlimited contributions. All they need to do is ask the campaign how their money ought to be spent—on what TV ads, for example. To prevent this, the FEC imposes restrictions on "coordination" between candidates, parties and groups making "independent expenditures." John Kerry alleges that the Swift Boat Veterans and the Bush campaign "coordinated" illegally. Republicans see similar ties between Kerry and Democratic 527s.

A Rise in Self-Censorship

But "coordination" is really "speech" and "political association." It's talking and planning among people who want to elect or defeat the same candidates. There's an indestructible inconsistency between the language of the First Amendment and campaign finance laws. Why shouldn't veterans coordinate with Bush? Why shouldn't Democratic 527s coordinate with Kerry? The Supreme Court upholds the campaign finance laws simply by ignoring the First Amendment's language.

All the legal twisting has (so far) produced mostly self-censorship. Politicians try to comply with the law's letter and evade its spirit. To maximize its support for Kerry, the Democratic National Committee [DNC] has set up a separate "independent expenditures" unit. The unit's top officials aren't supposed to talk politics with the Kerry campaign or other

2. The 2001 bill bans soft money to national political parties and bans state parties from using soft money in federal elections.

Federal Control of Speech

All [paid political] speech is subject to the overview and control of federal authorities. The FEC [Federal Election Commission] says such communications "must be paid for with federal funds meeting the limits, prohibitions and reporting requirements of the [Bipartisan Campaign Reform Act]. . . . The reporting obligations of state and local candidates making communication promoting, supporting, attacking or opposing federal candidates are governed by a number of provisions depending on the exact nature of the communications and the persons making them."

For running an ad that meets the definition of "electioneering communication," Americans running for public office in purely state and local elections are now subject to masses of red tape and regulation of the federal government. The failure of these state and local candidates to jump through these federal hoops could be construed as a criminal act. Any way you look at it, this is federal control of state and local candidates' political speech.

James O.E. Norell, *America's 1st Freedom*, December 2002.

DNC officials. In a recent *Newsweek* interview, DNC Chairman Terry McAuliffe was asked about the unit's ads. Here's his abbreviated (for space) response:

McAuliffe: Legally, I cannot have that conversation. . . . I cannot signal to the Kerry campaign what type of ads we're doing, how much money we're spending, because that would be deemed coordination. . . .

Q: You can't tell him anything about what the themes of your advertising will be?

A: No sir, absolutely not. . . .

Q: Do these rules strike you as absurd?

A: Yes.

Of course they're absurd. A party and its candidates should talk about whatever they want. If the First Amendment doesn't cover that, what would it cover? It's also unrealistic to think—regardless of legal precautions—that "signaling" won't occur between support groups and candidates.

A Choice Must Be Made

The media poorly describe what's happening. Campaign finance reform is a respectable cause. It's inconvenient to say that the First Amendment is being scalped. Few do. The *New York Times* recently ran a story on two campaign lawyers —one Democratic, one Republican—who bring cases before the FEC to bend "the complex rules to their clients' maximum benefit." The story barely hinted that, once candidates need lawyers and rulings to say what they can do, their constitutional protections have disappeared.

But the truth cannot remain forever obscured. Campaign finance laws must fail at their larger aim of improving public confidence in politics and government. They breed disrespect for law, the Constitution or both. If the laws are aggressively expanded and enforced—with more limits on contributions, spending and "coordination"—people will realize they're losing their rights of free speech and political association. But if the laws are laxly enforced, as they have been, they will inspire continuing evasions and harsh condemnations by "reformers." Public confidence suffers either way. Americans will ultimately have to choose between the Constitution and a mere law—or watch both be damaged.

> *"Any free air time system . . . should
> increase the flow of political information
> on the broadcast media."*

Candidates Should Be Given Free Air Time

Paul Taylor

In the following viewpoint Paul Taylor argues that free air time will improve political discourse by making it easier for all candidates, especially those from minor parties, to air advertisements. He outlines an approach that would grant qualifying candidates free advertising and require television and radio stations to devote a certain amount of time each week to broadcasting the candidates' views. According to Taylor, this proposal would help voters become better informed and enable challengers to better compete against well-financed incumbents. Taylor is the president of the Alliance for Better Campaigns, a public interest group that supports election reforms that make political communication more affordable, encourage voter participation, and promote more competitive elections.

As you read, consider the following questions:
1. What is the "lowest unit charge provision," as explained by Taylor?
2. According to Taylor, what variable best determines whether a political race will be competitive?
3. Why does Taylor compare television cameras to X-ray machines?

Paul Taylor, "The Case for Free Air Time," Alliance for Better Campaigns, March 2002. Copyright © 2002 by the Campaign Legal Center. Reproduced by permission.

In the area of political discourse, there are three laws on the books. A *reasonable access* provision requires that stations sell commercial air time to candidates who can afford to pay for it; an *equal opportunities* provision requires that stations which have sold spots to one candidate must provide his or her opponent with the chance to purchase comparable air time at a comparable price: and the *lowest unit charge* provision is supposed to assure that candidates will receive the same low rates as stations' best, year-round product advertisers.

There have been many proposals over the years to broaden these political discourse requirements to include mandatory free air time. The most recent was in 1998, when President [Bill] Clinton devoted a portion of his State of the Union speech to a call for the FCC [Federal Communications Commission] to adopt such a rule. "The airwaves are a public trust, and broadcasters also have to help us in this effort to strengthen our democracy," Clinton said. But the proposal never got out of the starting gate. Key congressional leaders who are friendly to the broadcast industry and averse to the idea of free air time going to their campaign opponents threatened to cut off appropriations to the FCC if it proceeded with a free air time rulemaking. In addition, the idea of having the FCC develop a free air time system was opposed by some congressional leaders, such as Sen. John McCain, who supported the concept but felt strongly that it should come about through legislation rather than regulation. In short order, the FCC backed off. With Clinton distracted that year by the Monica Lewinsky scandal and impeachment proceedings, the White House never put any political muscle behind its proposal. The closest it came to reviving the idea was later in the same year, when it appointed an advisory panel to update the public interest obligations of broadcasters in light of their recent grant of additional free spectrum to facilitate their transition to digital technology. Clinton and Vice President Al Gore made it clear they wanted the panel to develop a free air time proposal. But the 22-member panel had seven broadcast industry representatives on it, including panel co-chairman Leslie Moonves, the president of CBS Television. While all of the panel's 15 representatives of the public supported a free air time mandate, all of the broadcasters were opposed. In an effort to break the impasse and encourage some behavioral change among broadcasters, the panel came forward with a compromise. It recommended that television stations voluntarily air a minimum of five minutes a night of "candidate-centered discourse" in the month preceding all elections. With just a handful of exceptions, however, the nation's 1,300 local television stations roundly ignored this call for voluntary action. The typical local station aired just 45 seconds a night of candidate discourse in the month before the 2000 election—far short of the modest five-minute a night standard. Clearly, if there is to be behavioral change, it will have to come as a result of legislation rather than persuasion. . . .

One Approach to Free Air Time

Any free air time system should have two related—but distinct—objectives. It should reduce the cost of candidate communication and it should increase the flow of political information on the broadcast media. These goals are compatible, they are achievable, and they are constitutional. There are many different ways to structure a bill that would achieve these goals. Here is an outline of one possible approach:

I: A Voucher system for free political ads

The free air time system would provide vouchers for a reasonable amount of free advertising time to candidates and to political parties. The only candidates who would receive direct grants of vouchers would be those running for U.S. House and Senate seats in a general election who had first raised a threshold amount of contributions in small donations. In addition, each of the two major political parties would receive large block grants of broadcast vouchers in each election cycle—which the parties could use to air their own ads, or pass along for use by any general election candidate the party supported for any local, state or federal office. Minor parties that met qualifying thresholds would receive smaller blocks of free air time vouchers. The voucher system would be financed by a spectrum usage fee amounting to one half of one percent per year on the gross annual revenues of the nation's 1,300 local television station licensees and 13,000 local radio station licensees.

II: A Voters' time requirement

All television and radio licensees would be required to air a minimum of two hours a week of candidate discussion of issues in the month preceding every election. At least half of these segments would have to be aired in prime time or drive time. The formats would consist of debates, interviews, candidate statements, town hall meetings, mini-debates or any other similar news or public affairs programming of a broadcaster's choosing. Within these broad guidelines, all decisions about when the segments should air, how long they should be, what races they should focus on and what formats should be used would rest with local stations.

More Competitive and Informative Campaigns

Taken together, these two provisions would make political campaigns more informative and more competitive. They would be especially helpful to challengers, who often struggle to raise money and as a result have difficulty being heard by the broad public. By removing this barrier to entry, these provisions would open political campaigns up to the vitality that comes from fresh ideas, new candidates, and greater competition. But most of all, they would be helpful to the public. During the campaign season, citizens would receive a far richer diet of political information than they now get from television and radio. This would place them in a better position to cast an informed vote.

In the form outlined above, such a free air time system would not place limits on how much additional broadcast advertising a candidate could purchase. Some would argue that the absence of such a limit fatally detracts from the ability of the proposal to reduce the role of money in politics. There would be nothing, these critics would point out, to prevent well-financed candidates from airing a barrage of paid ads on top of the free ads they would air with their vouchers. Money would continue to dictate how loudly a candidate could speak. But others would argue that by at least providing a floor of communication resources to all candidates, this approach would help level the playing field. Research on campaign spending shows that the most important variable in determining whether a race will be competitive is not how much money the better financed candidate spends, but how much money the less well financed candidate spends. If that candidate, typically a challenger, has enough resources to get a hearing, he or she is in a much better position to make a strong race. Moreover, the "voters' time" provision of this free air time system would also provide opportunities for all candidates, regardless of the size of their campaign war chests, to get their message out over the airwaves in debates, issue forums, town hall meetings, etc. . . .

Making the Proposal Work

Should there be format restrictions on ads paid for with vouchers?

Very few. Many countries around the world impose format and/or content restrictions on free air time presentations, ranging from requirements that candidates appear in a studio setting to requirements that they refrain from attacking an opponent. But such restrictions would rub against the culture of unfettered political speech that has always been at the heart of our campaigns as well as our First Amendment. One way to promote desirable norms of accountability, substance and civility without resorting to onerous format restrictions might be to require that a simple statement appear at the bottom of every ad financed by a voucher: "This air time donated by the American people."

What will the "voters' time" segments look like?

It will be up to the broadcasters to figure this out. At their best, the segments will push candidates beyond spin and sound-bites. One attractive model is the one that has proven so durable on *Nightline*—after airing a short, well-balanced background report on a given issue, a skilled anchor leads two (or more) candidates though a spirited mini-debate. But there would also be value in using the time for interviews, footage from the day's stump speeches, debates, town hall meetings, etc. The television camera operates like an X-ray machine; the more exposure, the more likely it is that viewers will see through the masks that candidates sometimes wear. Let some segments run long, others short. Plug them into the regular nightly newscasts or run special public affairs programs right before the election. Let a thousand formats bloom. Eventually, someone is bound to figure out how to make good politics good television.

"Candidates should pay extra for running commercials that . . . poison the political process."

Candidates Should Not Be Given Free Air Time

Tom Peterson

In the following viewpoint Tom Peterson asserts that free air time proposals, which would provide qualified candidates with free TV advertising, will not solve the problems surrounding political advertising. He contends that the content, not the cost, of political commercials must be addressed. According to Peterson, candidates are wrongfully exempt from the standards of accuracy to which other advertisers must be held, a problem that free air time would not address. Peterson is a Louisville-based writer.

As you read, consider the following questions:
1. How do free commercials ordinarily benefit the public, according to Peterson?
2. What advertising rate must television stations give politicians, according to the author?
3. Why is Jim Carter, as quoted by Peterson, critical of free air time proposals?

Tom Peterson, "Free TV Ride for Politicians Should Get Derailed," *Louisville Eccentric Observer*, November 27, 2002, p. 16. Copyright © 2002 by the *Louisville Eccentric Observer*. Reproduced by permission.

Politicians have launched the next phase of campaign finance reform by proposing legislation that will provide them free air time on radio and television.

By reducing costs, the bill introduced by senators John McCain, R-Arizona; Russell Feingold, D-Wisconsin; and Richard Durbin, D-Illinois, is supposed to increase the flow of campaign communications and shine more light on issues.[1]

They are barking up the wrong tree.

Negative Ads Should Not Be Free

[In 2002] we've just finished the ugliest campaign season in memory. More candidates ran more negative campaign commercials than ever before. Now they want to pass a law so they can do that for less.

Do we want that?

Ordinarily, free commercials serve the public interest; spots donated by radio and TV stations promote community or charitable causes. They invite us to support or take advantage of organizations that support the common good.

I don't know about you, but I can't recall any campaign commercials from [the 2002] election that could be considered similarly uplifting or community spirited. . . . If anything, candidates should pay extra for running commercials that so poison the political process, as these did. But instead, they want to air them for free.

Standards Must Be Met

That won't solve any of the ills infecting our political process, because the problem isn't ad costs, it's the content. Candidates are exempt from the guidelines and restrictions regarding honesty and accuracy that all other advertisers must follow.

A political candidate can deliver to a TV station a commercial he knows to be false, misleading and unfair. Under current law, the TV station cannot refuse to run it. Not only that, the TV station must give the candidate the lowest rate available to its best advertisers.

If elected officials truly want to clean up campaigns, they

1. The bill had not come to a vote as of May 2005.

could do it tomorrow simply by agreeing to meet the standards met by all other advertisers. That doesn't require a law, just common sense. And it's free. Another reason for the proposed legislation is to limit the "windfall" profits broadcasters enjoy during election years.

An Alternative to Free Air Time

Free TV time for candidates is only the icing on a poisonously anti-competitive cake. If instead . . . we were to open up the TV band for all the wireless traffic it could accommodate, we would unleash an electronic explosion: scores of new (digital) TV stations and a plethora of innovations, including high-speed Internet access. The volcanic combustion of competitive entry would hurl new media conduits instantly within the consumer's reach. Speech would be cheaper, debate more robust, and citizens wouldn't even have to be herded up with TV "roadblocks" to become informed.

Thomas W. Hazlett, *Reason*, January 1997.

The Alliance for Better Campaigns says broadcasters nationwide took in more than $1 billion in campaign advertising during the 2000 campaign, the last election for which complete numbers are available. The organization says federally licensed broadcasters are making an unfair profit on democracy, and the "free time" is an appropriate give-back to communities they serve.

The Alliance's Web site (bettercampaigns.org) recently posted the dollars received by local TV stations for the 2002 campaign cycle. Kentucky television stations grossed more than $12.5 million from Jan. 1 through election day; Indiana stations took in slightly less, $10.7 million. The six Louisville-area stations made a combined $6.3 million, according to the Web site.

An Unconstitutional Proposal

The general managers of two local TV stations doubt the accuracy of the numbers but don't deny campaigns produce a lot of revenue. They challenge the notion that it's all "profit," given the costs of equipment, facilities and talent needed to put the spots on the air. They also believe the proposed legislation is not only unfair, but unconstitutional.

According to the Alliance Web site, WDRB-TV made more than $471,000 on political ads; its sister station, WFTE-TV, $33,000. WDRB general manager Bill Lamb says the figures represent about half of what the stations actually were paid for political advertising. He's also baffled by the lawmakers' interpretation of the Constitution.

"When the people who make the laws are the same people who benefit from the law, you create a huge conflict of interest," he said. "Besides, our viewers don't think there's a shortage of information out there, but they do believe there's too much negative campaigning."

The Slippery Slope of Free Air Time

WLKY-TV's general manager, Jim Carter, says the Alliance report—$2.1 million in campaign revenues for his station—is high. He also believes legislation that gives candidates free air time is the proverbial camel's nose under the tent.

"What's next—free airline tickets for candidates? If every industry regulated by the government is required to support the campaign process, they're voting themselves a free ride," he said.

Carter also challenges the fairness of a law that doesn't apply to all media. Unlike newspapers, which can add pages if advertising or news coverage demand it, TV and radio stations cannot add minutes to the day to accommodate "free" advertisers.

"A minute I have to give away to a candidate cannot be sold to another advertiser," Carter said. "How does locking out a retailer serve the common good?"

Free ads for campaigns aren't a good idea. The expense to our common sense and dignity is too high.

| *"Most of the information political ads do offer is of no use to the viewer."*

The Quality of Political Advertising Needs to Be Improved

Bill Hillsman

Political advertising is ineffective, Bill Hillsman contends in the following viewpoint. He asserts that if politicians want to inform voters, they must improve political commercials. According to Hillsman, these advertisements will be more effective if they become as creative as product ads, which do a much better job of engaging the audience. Hillsman is the president and chief creative officer at North Woods Advertising in Minneapolis, Minnesota.

As you read, consider the following questions:
1. In Hillsman's opinion why do political advertisements tend to look alike?
2. What is one of the basic rules of advertising that political consultants do not understand, according to the author?
3. According to Hillsman, what is the most troubling effect of negative advertising?

Bill Hillsman, "Commercial Fatigue: Why Bad Ads Happen to Good Voters," *Adweek*, vol. 45, March 29, 2004, p. 21. Copyright © 2004 by VNU Business Media. Reproduced by permission of the author.

Whenever the subject of political advertising comes up, that giant sucking sound you hear is presidential ads from years past. If there is any less effective and less efficient ad spending than that which goes on in presidential campaigns, I'm blissfully unaware of it. And based on the early evidence, expect the usual large doses of poorly produced propaganda and nasty character attacks this year [2004].

Both parties are working to solidify their base, and it's true that there are far fewer undecided voters than in years past. Nonetheless, a swing vote of between 3 million and 10 million independent voters will decide this election (and the majority of our competitive elections for the foreseeable future). Securing the base means close contact with the "customer": direct mail, phone calls, canvassing, volunteer recruitment, field organization, database mining and constant communications via the Internet. Persuading swing voters requires mass media. And that means advertising.

In the incumbent's corner, it's "Morning Again in America." George W. Bush's first ads were optimistic: we've been through a lot, but things are getting better. As anybody who's run a failing company knows, focusing on the future is a good strategy when you're stuck in a not-so-pretty present. Whether the president's ad makers can sell this message of optimism—even with the largest political ad budget in history—remains to be seen. In his second round of ads, Bush went negative.

In the other corner is the new JFK, John Forbes Kerry. Kerry's war-hero status is a strong contrast to George W. Bush's service record and a powerful antidote to the president's attempts to position himself as a wartime president. But Kerry, while not nearly as wooden as Al Gore, maintains a demeanor not often seen outside a mortuary. If he is to compete against Bush's massive budget, his ads will have to be much more effective than the usual political spots, and much more effective with independent voters than his spots have been so far.

How to Improve Political Ads

Political ads are so full of what-not-to-do's that the landscape would be immeasurably improved if they became simply average rather than risibly inept or egregiously insulting. So, to defend ourselves against still more putrid and stultifying political ads, here's a quick primer—an Advertising 101—for the practitioners of what I call Election Industry Inc.:

To be effective, an ad has to:

Get attention. Political ads fall miserably short of this goal, especially compared with product ads. Political ads are neither creative nor interesting enough to engage the viewer. And because of political consultants' innate desire to imitate rather than create, over time political ads in any given election cycle tend to look more and more alike and become less and less effective. Election Industry Inc. tries to get around this by making the ads ubiquitous and unavoidable—a strategy as futile for effective communications as it is profitable for political consultants (and a major reason why running for office is so costly).

Political ads are also hampered by poor production values. This immediately signals to viewers that the commercial is a political ad and will not be worth their time or attention. To summarize: what you're left with is advertising that is so ineffective and inefficient that it requires repeated airings just to be noticed by voters, who revile it once it's brought to their attention and then are subjected to it again and again. It's a poor way to make friends: You can't annoy someone into voting for your candidate.

Convey information. Political ads do a lousy job of this, too. It's not for lack of trying, or for lack of subject matter. Most political ads try to cram as much information as they can into 30 seconds. Somehow, political consultants have managed to not comprehend one of the most basic rules of modern advertising: each communication should have one specific point that the viewer or reader or listener will take away from the message.

Plus, most of the information political ads do offer is of no use to the viewer. Don't give me features; give me benefits. Don't tell me how a candidate voted, how many bills he or she passed, his or her position on an issue. Tell me how it made my life better.

Elicit a response. Most political communication is a one-way street: someone telling you what he or she wants you to

A Loss of Effectiveness

Political advertising is becoming less effective. In 1972 a General Electric study of televised advertisements found that the average person had to view an ad three times for it to sink in. This number is known as the "effective frequency." Over the years, as cable television and the Internet have flourished, viewers have become more difficult to reach, and advertisers now have a harder time getting them to remember ads. The effective frequency for consumer ads is now around five or six viewings. But political ads are even harder to remember— presumably because of their poor quality. Their effective frequency can run as high as twenty viewings. . . . Rather than come up with ads that are more memorable—more like consumer ads—campaigns have decided to pound viewers into distracted submission with the same mediocre product.

Joshua Green, *Atlantic Monthly*, July/August 2004.

hear. But communication by definition does not exist unless it goes two ways. Only then can a voter respond to a message or take action on it.

Turning Off Voters

Think of an ad as a transaction: You give me 30 seconds of your valuable time; I have to give you something back that you consider valuable. If I fail to do this, you will come away believing I wasted your time, and you will be that much less willing to give me 30 seconds of your attention next time. What can I give you that will make you feel the transaction is worthwhile? Any number of things. I could touch you emotionally. I could make you see something in a way you've never seen it before (a way you consider valuable). I could give you a new piece of information—information that you, not I, consider valuable. I could show you a demonstration of something you've never seen. I could make you laugh. When is the last time a political ad did anything like that for you?

Political advertising is over-polled, over-focus-grouped and over-copy-tested. Political ads do not involve the audience, they do not motivate the audience, and they do not get people to respond (other than to tune it out or turn it off). And the formulaic, often negative advertising championed by political consultants has an even more toxic effect: It dissuades voters from taking part in the election altogether, thereby turning the reins of our entire democratic process over to a highly motivated minority.

If this sounds negative, it's only a precursor to what might be the most negative presidential campaign of the last half-century. When the dust clears and one candidate limps to the finish, is it any wonder that our citizens remain polarized, and governing a united country becomes harder than ever?

It might be a stretch to say bad ads equal bad government, but it might not be as much of a stretch as you'd think.

> *"The most politically influential of all news
> media, television, has not taken well to the
> role of fact-checker."*

Television Journalists Need to Fact-Check Political Advertisements

Timothy Karr

Television news must do a better job of informing voters of inaccurate political commercials, Timothy Karr claims in the following viewpoint. According to Karr, television journalists are both unable and unwilling to devote sufficient time and resources to checking the facts of negative advertisements. He argues that the news media's failure to vet political ads ensures that many voters will be ill informed. Karr is the executive director of MediaChannel.org, a public interest Web site that provides information on the political and social impact of the media.

As you read, consider the following questions:
1. What worries Bob Garfield the most about televised political coverage, according to the author?
2. According to Karr, how do television journalists benefit when candidates attack one another?
3. What factors lead to high voter turnout, according to research by the *American Political Science Review*?

The political mud season is upon us [during the 2004 election] but many of those in the news industry that we have entrusted to sort out the mess are still leaning on their mops.

An early volley was launched [in March 2004] when President [George W.] Bush's reelection campaign released an ad accusing John F. Kerry of plans to raise taxes by $900 billion. Kerry's camp shot back with an ad that faults the Republican spot for "misleading America," and rebuts the president's tax claim against Kerry without going into specifics.

Both ads will run in at least 16 swing-voter states—from Pennsylvania to Florida to New Mexico—with the cash-rich Bush campaign buying three times as many slots as Kerry.

So, which ad is telling viewers the truth? That answer is difficult to find if one relies upon broadcast and cable news organizations to sort out the facts.

A Largely Silent Press

Many in television news haven't the resources to do the sort of investigative analysis of political attack ads that most voters need to make sense of the media melee. For one, the Bush ad claimed that Kerry, within his first 100 days, will "raise taxes by at least $900 billion" to "pay for new government spending." In a subsequent conference call with campaign press, Bush officials couldn't identify any Kerry statement regarding the $900-billion increase.

A more thorough analysis by healthcare analyst Ken Thorpe of Emory University revealed a complex calculus through which Kerry's plans for expanded health insurance coverage could result in federal costs of about $895 billion over ten years. Was the Republican accusation referring to this?

Most of the press stood mute; only a handful of print reporters, most notably Ronald Brownstein of the *Los Angeles Times*, put the numbers to the test. His analysis: "The Bush campaign's justification for the charge was specious. The Kerry campaign's response was misleading. And the vast press corps covering the campaign almost entirely failed to illuminate the holes in each side's arguments."

Commentators Tom Oliphant and David Brooks took

swipes at the Bush and Kerry spots during *Jim Lehrer's News Hour* on PBS. Their analysis, according to Brooks: "[The ads] wouldn't pass the standards Tom and I impose on ourselves."

Granted, voters can't always rely upon combative political campaigns to tell them the truth. But mainstream news reporters should step into the breach to decipher claims and separate truth from fiction. Unfortunately, the most politically influential of all news media, television, has not taken well to the role of fact-checker.

Titillation Instead of Education

"The major newspapers including the *New York Times, Los Angeles Times, Boston Globe* and the *Washington Post*, in general, do a good job of 'truth-squadding' political attack ads," said media commentator Bob Garfield, who is an ad critic for AdAge.com and the co-host of NPR's [National Public Radio's] *On the Media*. "But most of the smaller newspapers don't have the news hole or the resources for vetting these ads."

The problem according to Garfield is not with the printed press, but with television news, and in particular 24-hour cable news, that does not devote enough time to analysis of political attack ads.

"Cable news has been such a destructive force to reasoned analysis in an election year," said Garfield. "Its news appetite is voracious like a shark that only swims and eats. Cable news titillates voters but does very little to educate them."

What worries Garfield most is the political fallout from the medium's spread of negative candidate images. "People who vote are more heavily influenced by the allegations made in attack ads and not by any follow-up media reports that reveal the ads to be untrue," he said.

Shallow Descriptions

In their 1996 book, *Going Negative: How Political Advertisements Shrink and Polarize the Electorate*, Stephen Ansolabehere and Shanto Iyengar found that "most aspects of political campaigns are time-consuming to cover and don't make for good TV. In contrast to the standard campaign fare, 30-second spot ads contain great sound bites, arresting visuals, and sensational attacks, all in a package that fits easily into the two-minute format of television news."

Garfield sees an additional problem here. Wall-to-wall television news recycles image bites that often support thin characterizations of the candidates. We've seen it thus far [in 2004] in network news' portrayal of the Democratic primaries as a horse race pitting archetypal personalities against one another. [Howard] Dean was the mercurial candidate; John Kerry the aloof plutocrat, while John Edwards was the simple populist. This drama may have played well on the small screen, but it accomplished little towards educating voters about the candidates' political views. . . .

This was also the case in 2000 when, according to many political analysts, a well-funded Bush campaign successfully manipulated the media to cast Democratic nominee Al Gore as fundamentally dishonest and indecisive while tarring Republican opponent and decorated Vietnam veteran John McCain as unpatriotic.

"Based on coverage of Howard Dean, pre- and post-Iowa,[1] I see no evidence that television news has been chastened by the experience of 2000," Garfield said.

"TV is too compressed a medium to lay out the facts and reveal what is right and wrong," said Brooks Jackson, the founder of FactCheck.org, a non-partisan website that debunks misleading political statements. Jackson pioneered the "adwatch" and "factcheck" form of stories while a reporter at CNN. When CNN lost interest in slotting time for his reports, Jackson set up shop at the Annenberg Public Policy Center and launched his own political truth squad.

Since its launch in December 2003, many journalists have turned to FactCheck.org to vet political rhetoric when their own news organizations lacked the resources.

Jackson agrees with Garfield's assertion that untrue messages will resonate with voters despite the occasional media debunking of misleading political ads. "Because these campaigns are buying so much time, viewers will see their ads a hell of a lot more than they will see a news story about the ad. So it stands to reason that the ad makes a more lasting impression."

---

1. A clip of the candidate following the Iowa primary showing Dean screaming may have helped turn voters against him.

No Right to Refuse Political Ads

Some may wonder why political ads that contain falsehoods are allowed to air on television. Unlike commercial advertisers, who must adhere to a code of ethics and a set of regulations that stipulate truthfulness in advertisements, political advertisers are not accountable to any regulatory body, private or public, for the accuracy of their claims. Americans may thus be bombarded with inaccurate or unsubstantiated claims about the candidates.

Leah Haverhals, *World & I*, March 2001.

Angering the Electorate

For many TV journalists, it is a win-win situation when candidates attack one another. Broadcast news feeds on the images of conflict. In response campaign media strategists manufacture more negative portrayals of their rival, knowing well that broadcasters will be drawn to the flame. These negative "image-bites" can resonate even further with viewers, especially after the repeated viewings 24-hour news programming can provide.

"The electorate has been so turned off by attack ads that they might decide not to vote at all," warned Garfield.

Fewer voters are not always bad for campaigns, he added. "There is a silent conspiracy by both parties to make the political environment so distasteful that it creates a smaller electorate. It's easier to manage and manipulate a smaller constituency than it is to run a campaign that appeals to a larger population of voters."

The GOP strategy during the "Republican Revolution" of 1994, when Newt Gingrich allegedly fired up a voting block of "angry white men" to capture the House from the Democrats, featured one of the ugliest episodes of attack advertising in American history. The ads alienated large parts of the American electorate while, at the same time, energizing a core of white, male, Republican voters who turned out en masse for their candidates.

A Mixed Impact

According to Garfield, the Democrats are attempting to tap this same anger in 2004; in this case, to energize a core and unseat incumbent Bush. If this is true, voters shouldn't be shocked to see more negative campaign ads as the political mud season unwinds.

Jackson at FactCheck.org sees things differently. "I don't buy the idea that a low turnout is proof that campaigns were too divisive. Some of the most divisive campaigns sometimes attract the most voters." Research by the *American Political Science Review* suggests that campaigns characterized by lots of spending, uncertain outcomes, and active efforts by party and campaign organizations stimulate citizens to go to the polls.

When campaigns go negative, however, voters tend to peel away from the democratic process. And this is where the news media can step in, by motivating public participation in political issues and seeing that the campaigns address relevant topics accurately.

Whether they will in 2004 is a debate worth continuing. But it will require a lot more precision and care than the campaigns and newscasters displayed [in March 2004].

Periodical Bibliography

The following articles have been selected to supplement the diverse views presented in this chapter.

Whit Ayres	"Can Campaign Advertising Be on the Level?" *Campaigns & Elections*, October 2001.
E.J. Dionne Jr.	"The Radical Goal of McCain-Feingold's Enemies," *Liberal Opinion Week*, September 15, 2003.
Linda Feldman	"Political Ads: Cash Still King," *Christian Science Monitor*, August 25, 2004.
Joshua Green	"Dumb and Dumber: Why Are Campaign Ads So Bad?" *Atlantic Monthly*, July/August 2004.
Leah Haverhals	"Ignoring Distorted Political Ads," *World & I*, March 2001.
Nat Hentoff	"Supreme Court's Gag Rule on Us," *Village Voice*, January 28, 2004.
Jennifer G. Hickey	"Ads Treat Voters as Consumers," *Insight on the News*, November 12, 2002.
Mark Hosenball, Michael Isikoff, and Holly Bailey	"The Secret Money War," *Newsweek*, September 20, 2004.
Issues and Controversies On File	"Negative Campaign Advertisements," April 9, 2004.
Ruth Ann Weaver Lariscy and Spencer F. Tinkham	"Accentuating the Negative," *USA Today Magazine*, May 2004.
James O.E. Norell	"Free Speech in the Twilight Zone," *America's 1st Freedom*, December 2002.
Robert J. Samuelson	"A Marketing Revolution," *Newsweek*, August 9, 2004.
Alessandra Stanley	"Showing Candidates, as They Praise Themselves and Bury Others," *New York Times*, July 2, 2004.

CHAPTER 4

What Is the Future of Advertising?

Chapter Preface

One of the primary goals of advertising is to instill brand loyalty so that consumers will purchase specific products throughout their lives. Consequently, advertisers traditionally target children, teenagers, and adults in their twenties and thirties, in order to create customers who will be loyal for many decades. However, the demographics of the United States are rapidly changing as the sizable baby boomer generation approaches retirement age. With the U.S. population aging, many people argue that the advertising industry will need to change its focus and treat people in their fifties and beyond as a vital segment of the buying public.

Many commentators note that with the exception of a handful of campaigns, such as commercials for vitamins or other advertising that emphasizes active lifestyles, ads either ignore older Americans or portray them as feeble or absentminded. According to critics of these stereotypes, advertisers are disregarding the purchasing power of the middle-aged and elderly. In an article for the *Charlotte (N.C.) Observer*, Pam Kelley asserts, "Americans 50 and up are 38 percent of the population. By 2020, that jumps to 47 percent. . . . These people do spend money, and new research shows they switch brands and try new products."

Bolstering Kelley's views, the Bureau of Labor Statistics reports that purchases by Americans over the age of 55 represent 27 percent of the $4.2 trillion U.S. households spend on consumer goods each year. As the majority of this population is no longer raising children, older Americans can spend more disposable income on products that interest them, from cars to clothes to the latest technology. Media critic Marc Berman argues in *MediaWeek*, "Advertisers who ignore viewers aged 50-plus, or 54-plus, are missing households in which many of these so-called empty-nest 'geezers' suddenly discover they have some discretionary dollars. With the children grown, the same people who had been wearing shoes from Payless . . . now may be shopping for Gucci." As Berman suggests, brand loyalty is malleable for older Americans, a fact further supported by an American Association of Retired Persons study that found that Americans aged 45 years or older are as likely as those aged 18 to 34 to switch brands.

Whether advertisers will spend more of their budgets on appealing to older Americans remains to be seen, but there is little doubt that for advertisers to succeed in the future, they will need to adapt to a changing society. In the following chapter the authors evaluate the new forms that ads are taking and explore whether advertising will become too pervasive. Products may change, but the need to market them never will.

> *"Some of the traditional methods of advertising and marketing simply no longer work."*

Advertising Is Becoming Less Traditional

Economist

As traditional forms of advertising, such as commercials on television networks, become less effective, companies are adopting new approaches to marketing, the *Economist* asserts in the following viewpoint. According to the magazine, these less traditional types of advertising can include direct marketing, product placements, and telemarketing. The magazine also contends that Internet advertising will likely become more popular as well. The magazine concludes that as consumers are increasingly bombarded with commercials, it will become necessary for companies to find new ways to influence purchases. The *Economist* is a weekly financial magazine published in Great Britain.

As you read, consider the following questions:

1. According to the *Economist*, how much did it cost to air a thirty-second commercial during the 2004 Super Bowl?
2. By how much did Internet advertising revenues grow in the first quarter of 2004, compared with the first quarter of 2003, according to the magazine?
3. How many advertising messages do Americans see each day, as stated by the magazine?

It may have been Lord Leverhulme, the British soap pioneer, Frank Woolworth, America's first discount-retailer, or John Wanamaker, the father of the department store; all are said to have complained that they knew half of their advertising budget was wasted, but didn't know which half. As advertising starts to climb out of its recent slump, the answer to their problem is easier to find as the real effects of advertising become more measurable. But that is exposing another, potentially more horrible, truth for the $1 trillion advertising and marketing industry: in some cases, it can be a lot more than half of the client's budget that is going down the drain.

The advertising industry is passing through one of the most disorienting periods in its history. This is due to a combination of long-term changes, such as the growing diversity of media, and the arrival of new technologies, notably the internet. Consumers have become better informed than ever before, with the result that some of the traditional methods of advertising and marketing simply no longer work.

New Forms of Marketing

Ad spending grew rapidly in the late 1990s, but in 2000—just as the technology bubble was about to burst—it soared by more than 8% in America, which represents about half the world market. The following year it plunged by 8%. Spending is up again, according to ZenithOptimedia, which has long tracked the industry. It forecasts that worldwide expenditure in 2004 on major media (newspapers, magazines, television, radio, cinema, outdoor and the internet) will grow by 4.7% to $343 billion. It will be helped by a collection of big events, including the European football championship, the Olympic Games and an election in America. Historically, when there is an upturn in advertising expenditure, it tends to rise faster than the wider economy. So, provided economic growth can be sustained, ad spending may continue to pick up.

How will the money be spent? There are plenty of alternatives to straightforward advertising, including a myriad of marketing and communications services, some of which are called "below-the-line" advertising. They range from public relations to direct mail, consumer promotions (such as coupons), in-store displays, business-to-business promotions (like paying a retailer for shelf-space), telemarketing, exhibitions, sponsoring events, product placements and more.

These have become such an inseparable part of the industry that big agencies now provide most of them. Although some are less than glamorous, marketing services have grown more quickly than advertising. Add in the cost of market research, and this part of the industry was worth some $750 billion worldwide last year [2003], estimates WPP, one of the world's biggest advertising and marketing groups.

As ever, the debate in the industry centres on the best way to achieve results. Is it more cost-effective, for instance, to employ a PR agency to invite a journalist out to lunch and persuade him to write about a product than to pay for a display ad in that journalist's newspaper? Should you launch a new car with glossy magazine ads, or—as some carmakers now do—simply park demonstration models in shopping malls and motorway service stations? And is it better to buy a series of ads on a specialist cable-TV channel or splurge $2.2m on a single 30-second commercial during 2004's Super Bowl?

Such decisions are ever harder to make. Although a Super Bowl ad is still cheaper than in 2000, in general network-TV pricing has risen faster than inflation—even though fewer people tune in. Changes in TV-viewing habits, however, are only part of a much wider shift in the way media is consumed, not least because it has become more fragmented and diverse.

The Move Toward Internet Advertising

For a start, people are spending less time reading newspapers and magazines, but are going to the cinema more, listening to more radio and turning in ever-increasing numbers to a new medium, the internet.

After the technology bust it was easy to dismiss the internet. But the phenomenal success of many e-commerce firms, such as Amazon and eBay, shows that millions of people are becoming comfortable buying goods and services online. Many more are using the internet to research products, services and prices for purchases made offline. Some 70% of new-car buyers in America, for instance, use websites to determine which vehicle to buy—and often to obtain competing quotes from dealers.

Such consumers can be targeted by internet advertisers and, in some cases, their responses accurately measured. A surge in online advertising is being led by paid-for text-links dished up by search engines such as Google and Yahoo! The response rate from people clicking on paid links can be as low as 1%—about the same as direct mail, which remains one of the biggest forms of advertising. But there is an important difference: internet advertisers usually pay only if someone clicks on their link. This is the equivalent of paying for the delivery of junk mail only to households that read it.

Advertising on the Internet

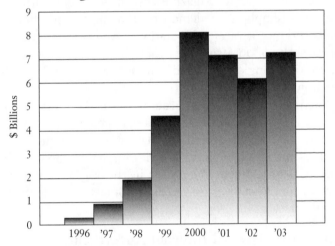

Interactive Advertising Bureau, 2003.

How are companies and the advertising industry responding to these trends in media consumption? Some people do not believe they amount to a sea-change, while others are simply hoping it will not come to pass on their watch, reckons Sir Martin Sorrell, WPP's chief executive. Nor is it the only significant force he sees at work. New markets, such as China, are becoming increasingly important for advertisers, especially multinationals. But these markets can have very different characteristics. Clients are also more concerned than ever about getting value for money. What will increasingly matter, says Sir Martin, is not what it costs to put an ad in front of 1,000 people (a traditional industry measure), but "how effective is that cost-per-thousand?"

At the same time, negotiating advertising deals is becoming tougher because of consolidation, both among clients and among media owners. This could favour the big, integrated agencies. In May [2004], WPP won a contract to handle all the advertising and marketing for HSBC [Hongkong and Shanghai Banking Corporation] after the international banking group decided that parent companies and not their individual agencies should bid for the $600m it spends on such services every year. Samsung, a big South Korean electronics firm, is also expected to appoint a single group.

Nevertheless, the smaller agencies believe they can still compete by being more nimble. "There is definitely a change in the landscape," says Jane Asscher, chairman of 23red, a London-based agency that describes itself as "media-neutral" in its choice of outlets for campaigns. Ms Asscher believes that consumers are becoming far more sophisticated in their reaction to all forms of advertising and marketing, so smarter ways have to be used to reach them.

During the slump, some companies tried different forms of advertising and liked the response they got. "There's lots of ways to skin a cat today," says Scott Goodson, founder of StrawberryFrog, an agency based in Amsterdam that specialises in international campaigns. While his firm still uses traditional media, such as TV and print, it is often in conjunction with other techniques, such as "viral" marketing. This means trying to spread the message by word of mouth—still considered the most-powerful form of advertising. Sometimes that involves using the internet for e-mail messages containing jokes, film clips and games, which recipients are encouraged to pass along to friends.

The Effectiveness of the Internet

No one knows just how important the internet will eventually be as an advertising medium. Some advertisers think it will be a highly cost-effective way of reaching certain groups of consumers—especially for small companies operating in niche businesses. But not everyone uses the internet, nor is it seen as particularly good at brand building. Barry Diller, the head of InterActiveCorp, believes network TV is a great place to promote his company's websites, such as Expedia, his online travel agency, and LendingTree, a consumer lender. Unlike bricks-and-mortar businesses, web-based firms do not worry if their ad is being seen by lots of people in towns where they have no shops. They just want people to remember their website address—or at least enough of their name to be Googled.

So far, the internet accounts for only a tiny slice of the overall advertising pie, although it has been growing rapidly. A joint study by the Interactive Advertising Bureau and PricewaterhouseCoopers found that internet advertising revenue in America grew by 39% to $2.3 billion in the first quarter of 2004, compared with the same period a year earlier. Internet ad revenues are now back above what they were at the height of the tech boom.

And Google and Yahoo! have yet to unleash the full potential of their technology. Google, which already places text ads on other people's websites and splits the revenue with them, recently began testing a system to distribute display ads as well, in effect increasing its role as a sort of online ad agency.

Honing New Technologies

Others are honing new techniques. As part of a recent campaign for American Airlines, the online edition of the *Wall Street Journal* used "behavioural targeting" to estimate how likely readers were to be frequent-flyers based on how much interest they paid to travel-related stories and columns. The targeted readers were presented with American Airline ads, and not just when they were reading travel stories. According to Revenue Science, a New York company that developed the targeting system, the results were dramatic: the number of business travellers who saw the ads more than doubled.

The potential for advertising on the internet is tempting

more firms to join the fray. For instance, Microsoft is working on a search system with the intention of leapfrogging Google. Microsoft and others see that as more types of media, including music and films, start to be distributed over the internet, there will be more opportunities for online operators to put advertising messages in front of consumers.

Indeed, the makers of personal video recorders (PVRs) recently announced that their new machines will be capable of downloading music and films from the internet, as well as from TV. Many advertisers dread PVRs because they can be used to "time shift" viewing, allowing viewers to record their own schedules with greater ease than existing video recorders. Several studies have shown that users think one of the machine's most-appealing features is the ability to skip past ads. The providers of internet-based content might be able to slip in those ads in other ways than traditional 30-second commercials, perhaps through sponsorship deals or as display ads on the websites which PVR owners will use to select their programming.

An Attack of Advertisements

People are tiring of ads in all their forms. A recent study by Yankelovich Partners, an American marketing-services consultancy, says that consumer resistance to the growing intrusiveness of marketing and advertising has been pushed to an all-time high. Its study found 65% of people now feel "constantly bombarded" by ad messages and that 59% feel that ads have very little relevance to them. Almost 70% said they would be interested in products or services that would help them avoid marketing pitches.

It has been calculated that the average American is subjected to some 3,000 advertising messages every day. If you add in everything from the badges on cars to slogans on sweatshirts, the ads in newspapers, on taxis, in subways and even playing on TVs in lifts [elevators], then some people could be exposed to more than that number just getting to the office. No wonder many consumers seem to be developing the knack of tuning-out adverts.

"Consumers are getting harder to influence as commercial clutter invades their lives," says a recent report by Deutsche

Bank. It examined the effectiveness of TV advertising on 23 new and mature brands of packaged goods and concluded that in some cases it was a waste of time. Although in the short-term TV advertising would lead to an incremental increase in volume sales in almost every case, there was only a positive cash return on that investment in 18% of cases. Over a longer term the picture improved, with 45% of cases showing a return on investment. Not surprisingly, new products did better than older ones. The study concluded that "increased levels of marketing spending were less important than having new items on the shelf and increasing distribution."

The effectiveness of advertising is a hugely controversial area. Conventional wisdom in the industry is that sales may well increase for a certain period even after the advertising of a product ends. But there comes a point when sales start to decline and it then becomes extremely expensive to rebuild the brand.

Conventional Wisdom Is No Longer True

This supports the idea of continuous advertising. But some people in the industry believe the conventional wisdom is no longer true. When America's big TV networks reached prime-time audiences of 90% of households, they were a powerful way to build a brand. Now that those audiences might be as low as one-third of households, other ways of promoting a brand have become more competitive. Moreover, many clients never really embraced continuous advertising: when times get tough, just as they did after 2000, one of the first things many companies cut is their ad budget.

Robert Shaw, a visiting professor at the Cranfield School of Management in Britain, runs a forum in which a number of big companies try to monitor the "marketing payback" from advertising. The return from traditional media was, he says, "never terribly good". Generally under half of ads provide a return on their investment. And there can be various reasons why ads influence sales, other than their direct effect on consumers. For instance, if a producer announces a multi-million dollar ad-campaign, then retailers are often persuaded to increase deliveries. This can result in a "distribution effect" that leads to additional sales.

Some companies have profited from re-allocating their spending across different media, adds Mr Shaw. But it is a tricky business to determine what works best. For many companies, and especially the media-buyers who purchase space and slots for ads, greater media diversity and the arrival of the internet has made a difficult job much tougher. . . .

Reinventing Advertising

Despite all of these complications, many in the advertising business remain sanguine. For Rupert Howell, chairman of the London arm of McCann Erickson, which is part of the giant Interpublic group, the industry's latest downturn was the third he has experienced. As it did from the others, he says, the industry is emerging a little wiser. But, he insists, "the underlying principles haven't changed." Even the arrival of new media, like the internet, does not spell the demise of the old. Indeed, as he points out, TV never killed radio, which in turn never killed newspapers. They did pose huge creative challenges, but that's OK, he maintains: "The advertising industry is relentlessly inventive; that's what we do."

> "*[Major advertisers] are shifting resources away from traditional advertising and toward more hidden product placement.*"

Product Placement Is Becoming Too Ubiquitous

Bonnie Erbe

In the following viewpoint Bonnie Erbe asserts that the use of product placements in movies and television has made advertising more inescapable. According to Erbe, the appearance of specific brands of food, cars, and other items in these programs is upsetting because viewers are unable to avoid such advertising. She contends that consumers must be on guard for these hidden commercials. Erbe is a syndicated columnist.

As you read, consider the following questions:

1. According to the author, what was one of the earliest examples of product placement?
2. Why are some product placements free, according to Erbe?
3. How much money did Philip Morris spend on promotional expenditures in the last quarter of 2002, according to Erbe?

L et us now skewer a new advertising-industry technique for so thoroughly concealing itself as to trick us into believing some ads don't exist. The trickery I'm referring to is called "product placement."

The average American consumer is pounded daily by ads in newspapers, on television, on radio, at bus stops and train stations, via roadside billboards, in Internet pop-ups and recorded telemarketing spiels. Ads, ads—they're everywhere. But a much more venal form of capitalism's unwanted stepchild (the relentless pitch) has grown in use and efficacy to the point where advertising as we know it is falling from favor.

A Half-Century of Product Placement

Product placement is a more venal (and subliminal) pitch mode. Advertisers traditionally procure an annoying but nonetheless legitimate marketing segment that is separate and distinct from the entertainment vehicle in which it airs. Now, advertisers have found they might penetrate your subconscious all the more stealthfully by placing products in the content portions of those programs.

This mendacious trend apparently started in the movies. One of the earliest examples dates back a half-century when, HowStuffWorks.com notes, "Gordon's Gin paid to have Katharine Hepburn's character in 'The African Queen'" toss loads of its product overboard. Since then, there have been countless placements in thousands of movies. In fact, surreptitious sales pitches are so ubiquitous, the trailer for the movie, "Josie and the Pussycats" spoofed the practice. It squeezed "placed" products from all the following companies into a two-minute time frame, according to HowStuffWorks.com: "America Online, American Express, Bebe, *Billboard Magazine*, Bugles, Campbell's Soup, Coke, *Entertainment Weekly Magazine*, Evian, Ford, Gatorade, Kodak, Krispy Kreme, McDonald's, Milky Way, Motorola, Pepperidge Farm Cookies, Pizza Hut, Pringles, Puma, Ray-Ban, Sega, Starbucks, Steve Madden, Target and T.J. Maxx."

Not all product placements are purchased. Some come free of charge in exchange for providing a studio or network with badly needed props at the last minute. Yes, so cunning and sadly successful is the scheme, of late it has expanded beyond Hollywood. At least in movies, it could be argued, no consumer so much as expects reality, honesty or even most times, intellectual rigor.

The Effects of Product Placement on Children

Children ages 10 to 15 who watch more than five hours of television per week are six times more likely to begin smoking cigarettes than those who watch less than 2 hours per week. Another prominent tactic . . . is the strategic positioning of billboards and signs during sports programming. This is a prime spot to push alcohol products to a young audience who are frequent viewers of athletic events and are difficult to reach with traditional advertising methods.

Rod Gustafson, *Parenting and the Media*, April 6, 2004.

Now advertisers are venturing into other media. A recent *Wall Street Journal* interview promoted a rising network executive star who gushed shamelessly about her cross-platform product-placement powers (the woman is in charge of placing products on a variety of co-owned broadcast and cable networks as well as other media).

Ignoring Hidden Advertisements

Call me crazy, but I prefer to know when I'm some ad agency's target of opportunity. I need to know so I can ignore the message. I need to know so I can vent my resentment. I need to know so I can go out of my way NOT to patronize the brand or product that invaded my space. I need to know so I can buy the generic version (if one's available).

Then I'm secure in the knowledge no one's exaggerated the capabilities of my small-dollar purchase (cleans all surfaces, relieves cold symptoms, etc.). I rest easier knowing my money is not subsidizing the exorbitant salary of some Madison Avenue sorcerer who is owed as little toward that product's success as the Wizard of Oz was for getting Dorothy back to Kansas (and we all know the curtain was pulled on the Wizard's lame shamanics, too).

Major advertisers are beginning to understand that consumers don't trust ads. Some are shifting resources away from traditional advertising and toward more hidden product placement or feel-good promotion.

The Gallup Organization noted in a 2002 Web posting, "There is mounting evidence that leading companies may be questioning the role of advertising and the amounts they have been spending on it. Mega-advertiser Philip Morris recently announced that, rather than increase its advertising budget, it would greatly increase its promotional expenditures in the fourth quarter of this year, adding $600–650 million on top of an already announced $350 million targeted for price promotions."

As that happens, we as consumers and as targets need to be on guard for the barrage of hidden sales pitches, so we can inure ourselves to them, as we are inuring ourselves to the obvious ones.

| "The problem of spam may be a technical arms race."

The Proliferation of Internet Spam Will Require Creative Solutions

Wendy M. Grossman

The use of junk e-mails, or "spam," to advertise products is a serious problem that must be solved, Wendy M. Grossman maintains in the following viewpoint. According to Grossman, possible solutions include e-mail filters and fees for sending e-mails. However, she argues, the most effective approach may be for the Internet community to work together on a technical scheme to block spam. Grossman is the author of *From Anarchy to Power: The Net Comes of Age.*

As you read, consider the following questions:
1. According to the author, what percentage of her incoming e-mail is spam?
2. According to Grossman, what is the basic economic solution to junk e-mails?
3. In the author's view, what does the Usenet experience illustrate?

Junk e-mail is like seasickness: If you don't get it, you don't really understand how bad it is. In 1997, when I proposed my first article on spam, the English editor I approached insisted it was an "American problem." One of his colleagues and I convinced him to take it seriously by ganging up on him: For a week we both sent him a copy of every piece of junk we received.

We couldn't do that now. Heavy Internet users can get hundreds of these messages every day. America Online reported in March that the company filters an average of 22 junk e-mail messages a day per account—up to 780 million per day. Brightmail, which supplies spam-blocking services and products to Internet service providers (ISPs) and enterprises, counted 1.9 million spam campaigns in November 2001, 7 trillion in April 2003. By June 2003, the company says, spam was 48 percent of Internet e-mail traffic, up from 8 percent in January 2001.

Spam volume is likely to grow further: The longer people are on the Net, the more spam they tend to receive. Aggregating all of my addresses, some of which get no junk and some of which get nothing else, 56 percent of my incoming e-mail is already spam. . . .

The Problem of Spam

The chief reason people send spam is that it's incredibly cheap to do so. The response rates are tiny compared to those seen in other types of direct marketing, but there are no printing costs, minimal telecommunications costs, almost no labor costs, and no publisher reviewing the content of your ad. It is, to be sure, socially unacceptable behavior. ISPs that let people send spam through their servers may find themselves blacklisted and their customers' e-mail blocked by other ISPs, and companies who send it themselves or who hire third parties to do it for them may find themselves boycotted.

One of the key objections to banning spam is that it amounts to censorship: No one, the argument goes, should have the right to interfere with a person's private e-mail or decide who can or cannot send e-mail or what it may contain. What is often forgotten is that spam itself can be a form of censorship. Many e-mail services have limits on the amount of e-mail that can be stored in a user's inbox at one time. Fill up that space with an unexpected load of junk, and wanted e-mail gets bounced.

Similarly, consider the advice that's often given to people to help avoid getting on the spammers' lists: Hide your e-mail address. The advice makes some sense. In March [2003] the Center for Democracy and Technology released the results of a six-month study on how spammers get people's addresses; the most popular method was to harvest them from Usenet or the Web. But hiding addresses has many undesirable social consequences. If there's no visible e-mail address, you can't tell someone there's an error on his Web site or ask for more information. Businesses have to choose between making staff less accessible and making e-mail less productive. . . .

Technical Solutions

Most solutions to spam fall into three classes: technical, economic, and legal. All three have major drawbacks, and even without those none would provide a total solution.

The technical solutions are probably the most familiar because they're the things you can do for yourself. Primarily, these solutions involve filtering the junk out of the stream of e-mail. There are several places along the path from sender to recipient where filtering can be carried out: at the sending ISP, at the receiving ISP, and through the recipient's own e-mail software. Early in the Internet's history, any mail server was available to send e-mail on behalf of any user: You just specified the machine in your e-mail software, and the server relayed the mail for you. When junk e-mail became a problem, these relays were one of the first things to go. Running an open relay, once seen as a social contribution, became socially irresponsible. The cost was that closing those relays down made it more difficult for travelers and guests to send e-mail while out of range of their own systems.

A number of ISPs offer filtering services for their customers using a third-party service like Brightmail or Spam-Assassin, and these vary from discarding the junk on your behalf to marking suspected junk in such a way that you can set your e-mail software to filter it into a separate location. The advantage to the first scheme is that you never see the junk; the advantage to the second is that you can see what's being discarded, and if a legitimate message is incorrectly marked you have a way of retrieving it.

San Francisco's conferencing system the WELL employs the second approach; it uses SpamAssassin, which marks the junk for filtering. SpamAssassin assigns a score to each message that in its estimation indicates the likelihood that the message is spam. A Web interface provided by the WELL lets users set the threshold above which the message is marked. At the default settings, the WELL's implementation catches about two-thirds of the junk. It's not enough: WELL accounts tend to attract a lot of spam even if they haven't been used outside the WELL itself.

Lane. © 2003 by *The Baltimore Sun*. Reproduced by permission of Cagle Cartoons, Inc.

At the user level, a number of companies make plug-ins for standard e-mail software, some free, some commercial. These sit between your e-mail software and your ISP, and examine your messages as they arrive, marking or deleting anything they can identify as spam. Internally, they all work slightly differently. Some of these filters check the origins of messages against one or more Realtime Blackhole Lists and eliminate anything that comes from known spam-tolerant ISPs. These blacklists do weed out a lot of junk, but again there's a price, since it's always possible for an innocent domain to get listed by mistake or malice. Of course, the same is true of system administrators who put filters in place; they've been known to block whole countries (including the U.K.). . . .

Economic Solutions

From time to time, someone proposes an economic solution to spam. There are a number of variations, but they all boil down to one idea: You should pay, literally, for all the e-mails you send. This is a popular idea because even a tiny charge that wouldn't cost individual users very much would impose a substantial burden on spammers. At a penny per e-mail, for instance, sending 1 million messages would cost $10,000. At the very least, such a fee would get spammers to clean their lists.

There are several problems with this idea. First and foremost, no ISP in the world is set up to charge this way. It would require an entirely new infrastructure for the industry. In addition, charging for e-mail would kill free services such as Yahoo! and Hotmail in a single stroke and, with greater social costs, make today's many valuable mailing lists economically unfeasible. If we had micropayments—that is, the technical ability to manage transactions of a penny or even fractions of a penny—we'd have more flexibility to consider charging schemes with fewer social costs. If, for example, you could require that unknown correspondents attach one cent to an e-mail message, you could void the payment for wanted e-mail, leaving only the spammers to pay it.

Legislative Solutions

But we don't have micropayments and we have little immediate prospect of getting them. Given the costs to the industry of altering its billing infrastructure, the only way a pay-per-message scheme would work is if it were legally mandated—and even then, such a mandate could not be imposed worldwide. In one of the biggest turnarounds in Net history, many people who formerly opposed the slightest hint of government regulation online are demanding anti-spam legislation. So far, the European Union has made spam illegal, 34 states in the U.S. have banned it, and a number of competing federal bills are in front of Congress, which has considered such legislation before. Various proposed federal laws would require spam to include labels, opt-out instructions, and physical addresses; to ban false headers; to establish a do-not-mail registry; or to ban all unsolicited advertising. Most of the state laws require labeling and opt-out mechanisms.

Not everyone is happy with the U.S. legislation's provisions, however: Steve Linford, head of Europe's Spamhaus Project, says America's opt-out approach will legalize flooding the world with spam. He notes that the world's 200 biggest spammers are all based in Florida. With an opt-out system, anyone would have the right to put you on any list at any time, as long as they remove you if you request it. Linford believes instead that "opt in"—prohibiting companies from adding addresses to lists unless their owners have given their specific consent—is the key to effective anti-spam legislation.

Whatever the merits of Linford's and others' proposals, there's an important point to remember: None of the anti-spam laws passed so far has been effective, and that's not likely to change. . . .

The Usenet Solution

There's one more approach to the spam problem that we should consider. For the lack of a better term, we might call it the community solution. Alternatively, we could call it the Usenet approach.

Created in 1979, Usenet is in many respects still the town square of the Internet. It played that role even more in 1994, when the Web was still in its "before" stage and two Arizona lawyers, Martha Siegel and Laurence Canter, sent out an infamous spam advertising their services, provoking a furious reaction. The technical method used to post the message meant that you couldn't mark it read in one newsgroup and then not see it in the others, so anyone reading a number of Usenet newsgroups saw the message in every single group.

When the uproar eventually settled, a new hierarchy of ad-friendly newsgroups was created, each beginning with the prefix "biz." But this approach never really worked, because the kind of people who advertise anti-cellulite cream, get-rich-quick schemes, and cable descramblers don't care if they annoy people; they just want maximum eyeballs. In the ad hoc newsgroup news.admin.net-abuse.usenet, users and administrators discussed and developed a system that took advantage of the cancellation features built into Usenet's design. These are primarily designed so people can cancel their own messages, but a number of public-spirited people hacked them so third parties could use them to cancel spam.

By now spam has died out in many newsgroups, partly because the system worked and partly because the spammers simply moved to e-mail's wider audience. But the worst spam period cost Usenet many of its most valuable and experienced posters, who retreated to e-mail lists and more private forms of communication and have never come back.

Creating Community Standards

The key to making this system work was community standards that defined abuse in terms of behavior rather than content. Spam was defined as substantively identical messages, posted to many newsgroups (using a threshold calculated with a mathematical formula) within a specified length of time. The content of the message was irrelevant. These criteria are still regularly posted and can be revised in response to community discussion. Individual communities (such as newsgroups run by companies or ISPs) can set their own standards. It is easy for any site that believes canceling spam threatens free speech to block the cancels and send an unfiltered newsfeed.

The issues raised by Usenet spam were identical to those raised by junk e-mail today. The community, albeit a much smaller one, managed to create standards supported by consensus, and it came up with a technical scheme subject to peer review. A process like this might be the best solution to the spam e-mail problem. The question is whether it's possible given the much more destructive techniques spammers now use and given the broader nature of the community.

Some working schemes for blocking spam are based on community efforts—in which the first recipients of a particular spam send it in, for example, so it can be blocked for other users in the group. In addition, the Net has a long tradition of creating tools for one's own needs and distributing them widely so they can be used and improved for the benefit of all. As in the Usenet experience, there is very little disagreement on what spam is; that ought to make it easier to develop good tools. I can't create those tools, but I can offer less technical friends a spam-filtered e-mail address on my server, which has SpamAssassin integrated into it (after a month of work to get it running), to help them get away from the choked byways of Hotmail or AOL. If everyone with the technical capability to run a server offered five friends free, filtered e-mail, many consumers would be able to reclaim their inboxes. Some ISPs are beginning to offer—and charge for—such a service.

In the end, the ISPs are crucial to this fight. In the Usenet days, system administrators would sometimes impose the ultimate sanction, the Usenet Death Penalty—a temporary block on all postings from an ISP that had been deaf to all requests to block spam sent from its servers. It usually took only a couple of days for the offending ISP to put better policing in place—the customers would demand it. That's what the Realtime Black-hole Lists do, constructing their databases of known spam sources from pooled reports. But the bigger and richer ISPs such as Hotmail and AOL, can take the lead by taking legal action, as they are beginning to do. AOL filed five anti-spam lawsuits [in spring 2003] alone.

Winning the Spam War

The Usenet experience shows that the Net can pull together to solve its own problems. I don't think we're anywhere near the limits of human technical ingenuity to come up with new and more effective ways of combating spam, any more than I think e-mail is the last electronic medium that spammers will use. (There have been a couple of cases of "blogspam," where robot scripts have posted unwanted advertising to people's blogs.) The problem of spam may be a technical arms race, but it's one that's likely to be much easier to win than a legislative arms race.

When I spoke with Danny Meadowes-Klue, head of the U.K.'s Interactive Advertising Bureau, he told me, "Spam is the biggest threat to the Internet." But he didn't mean what you think he meant. He was talking about the destructiveness of so many efforts to stop it.

"Advertising itself is far too narrow a concept to encompass the effects of the rampant commercialism that now confronts us."

Advertising Is Becoming Too Pervasive

Robert W. McChesney and John Bellamy Foster

Advertising is taking over nearly every element of society, Robert W. McChesney and John Bellamy Foster opine in the following viewpoint. They argue that the amount of advertising heard or seen on radio and television has exploded in recent years. In addition, the authors maintain that advertisers are gaining more control over the editorial content of television shows and magazines and are also using movies and music to spread their messages. The authors conclude that this massive leap in commercialism is destroying American culture. McChesney and Foster are editors for the magazine *Monthly Review*.

As you read, consider the following questions:
1. According to the authors, advertising accounted for how many minutes of prime time programming in 2002?
2. In McChesney's and Foster's opinion, what is the new paradigm for media and commercialism?
3. What is the logic of corporate advertising, as explained by the authors?

Robert W. McChesney and John Bellamy Foster, "The Commercial Tidal Wave," *Monthly Review*, vol. 54, March 2003. Copyright © 2003 by the Monthly Review Press. Reproduced by permission.

A dvertising is part of the bone marrow of corporate cap-italism. Yet it does not happen on its own. It requires advertising-friendly policies and regulations to allow it to flourish. Once these conditions are established it becomes a self-propelling system. Advertising has become such a dom-inant source of revenue for the media industries that those media outlets that do not attract advertising find themselves at a decided disadvantage in the marketplace. Advertising thus becomes ever more ubiquitous. One of the ironies of advertising in our times is that as commercialism increases, it makes it that much more difficult for any particular ad-vertiser to succeed, hence pushing the advertiser to even greater efforts. Many in advertising are not necessarily ex-cited by the push to increase commercialism—sometimes they are downright critical of the effect on culture—but feel powerless to challenge it. "It's the ultimate challenge," one ad executive stated in 2000. "The greater the number of ads, the less people pay attention to them. One ad is the same as another now. People simply don't believe them anymore." The declining effectiveness of individual ads as overexposed consumers develop immunities, has become a source of real concern for marketing firms, which find themselves forced to run faster and faster just to stand still. In the words of David Lubars, a senior ad executive in the Omnicom Group, consumers "are like roaches—you spray them and spray them and they get immune after a while." The only answer is to spray them some more.

The Onset of Hypercommercialism

The resulting commercial tidal wave assumes many forms. On the one hand, it means that traditional commercial me-dia are increasing the amount of advertising. Radio advertis-ing has climbed to nearly 18 or 19 minutes per hour, well above the level [of] only a decade earlier. Television has been subjected to a similar commercial marination. Until 1982, commercial broadcasters operated under a nonbinding self-regulatory standard of no more than 9.5 minutes per hour of advertising during prime-time and children's programming. Even with that standard commercial broadcasters were lam-basted for carpet-bombing the population with ads. However, today that looks like a veritable noncommercial Garden of Eden. By 2002, advertising accounted for between 14 and 17 minutes per hour of prime time programming on the major networks, easily an all-time high. The amount of time devoted to advertising on television during prime time grew by more than 20 percent between 1991 and 2000. Popular programs like *The Drew Carey Show* had over 9 minutes of advertising over a half-hour. And that's not the half of it. In addition to the amount of commercial time increasing, the shorter 15-second spot, which barely existed in the 1980s, has come to account for nearly a third of the commercial time on TV. So the total number of ads increased even more dramatically. Broadcasters took advantage of new digital compression technologies to "squeeze" programs down in length to insert even more advertising. The quest to commercialize the airwaves was pushing to new frontiers. Digital ads were inserted into baseball telecasts, visible during the game itself. The UPN Network even proposed running onscreen advertisements during its programs.

The Destructive Effects of Marketing

One of the many problems with a culture based on relentless advertising and hyperconsumerism is the grim environmental effect. Accordingly to the most recent estimate by Mathis Wackernagel, the author of *Our Ecological Footprint*, if everyone consumed at the level of the average North American, it would take four extra planets to provide the necessary resources to survive. Globalization and the marketing of the American consumer lifestyle provokes millions of global consumers to suddenly "need" sport utility vehicles, big screen TVs and closets of stuff—something the already overburdened planet can ill-afford. Perhaps the prophecy of the nineteenth century writer William Dean Howells will be correct, that "there will presently be no room in the world for things; it will be filled up with the advertisements of things."

Anna White, *Enough!* no. 8, 1999.

All of this hypercommercialism leaves advertisers frustrated, as their particular messages are more likely to get lost in the shuffle, but their recourse invariably is to ratchet up the sales effort accordingly. It also infuriates viewers, who do whatever they can to avoid the commercial onslaught. New technologies, such as digitalized personal video recordings, make this considerably easier, much to the dismay of media executives. "You're getting to the stage where television advertising in certain product sectors and to certain target groups simply becomes wallpaper," one ad executive stated in 2002, "and even if you did spend more on it, it wouldn't work." The immediate solution to this problem has been a massive increase in "product placement" in entertainment programming, where the product is woven directly into the story so it is unavoidable, and its message can be smuggled in when the viewer's guard is down. Coca-Cola, for example, paid $25 million dollars to AOL Time Warner so that, among other things, characters in the WB Network's "Young American" series would "down Cokes in each episode.". . .

Taking Over Editorial Content

The long-standing notion of the separation between the advertising and editorial/creative sides of media is rapidly crumbling. To some extent this is due to ad clutter, and to some extent it is due to new ad-skipping technologies, but mostly it is due to the greed of media companies desperate to attract commercial support. The clout of large advertisers has grown; approximately 80 percent of U.S. ad spending is funneled through the eight largest companies that own advertising agencies, like Omnicom or Interpublic, which gives them considerable ability to name their tune with corporate media firms more than willing to play ball. "The tables have turned," Wendy's marketing chief stated in 2002. If media firms do not accommodate their wishes, "marketers will take their ad dollars to other places. There are too many ways to reach consumers." Accordingly, Wendy's was able to have Rosie O'Donnell tout Wendy's salads during an episode of her talk show, and eat one of the salads on air. The list goes on and on. The USA Network held top-level "off-the-record" meetings with advertisers in 2000 to let them tell the network what type of programming content they wanted in order for USA to get their advertising. "The networks didn't use to want us," the J. Walter Thompson executive in charge of Ford's TV account stated in 2002. "I sense a sea change.

. . . I've been amazed by people's willingness to write [Ford] into scripts. I've had to remind them to keep it entertaining." AOL Time Warner's TNT cable channel sent out an open call to advertisers in 2000, in an effort to get products placed in all its programs wherever possible. Comcast's G4 game show TV channel offered advertisers an opportunity to have their commercial appear as part of the programs. As a G4 executive said to advertisers, "If you have an idea, we'll play."

A Return to the Early Days

In a sense this is a return to broadcasting's early days, when advertisers actually produced the programs that went on the air. And, fittingly enough, soap operas have rapidly embraced the explicit commercialization of editorial content. In 2002 Revlon was given a prominent role in Disney-owned ABC's "All My Children" in exchange for millions of dollars in advertising. But what is happening now goes far beyond what was done from the 1930s to the 1950s in radio and television, in both scope and intensity. It is the media firms that are leading the push, now, and they are most definitely pushing the commercial envelope. "As the competition for ad dollars intensifies," one Disney-owned ESPN executive stated, "we are exploring alternative ways to give advertisers added value for their time. We have to think outside the box." ESPN has begun work on "long-form" commercials where products are integrated into entertaining segments on sport. In 2002 ABC's "Monday Night Football" featured ads with announcer John Madden that were virtually indistinguishable from the program itself. News Corporation's cable television sports show "The Best Damn Sports Show Period" assumed by 2003 the "leading role in blurring the boundaries between advertising and programming," when it made the mascot for its largest advertiser, Labatt beer, a recurring character on the program. By 2002 commercial broadcasters were gearing up to develop "ebay-TV," whereby direct selling of products could be done in conjunction with programming. The media firms claim all this commercial involvement has no influence over actual media content, but this claim fails to pass even the most basic giggle test, it is so preposterous. "Who are they kidding," the *Los Angeles Times* TV columnist wrote in 2002.

"Why would companies pony up cash without expecting some input over how it is spent?"

In sum, we are rapidly moving to a whole new paradigm for media and commercialism, where traditional borders are disintegrating and conventional standards are being replaced with something significantly different. It is more than the balance of power shifting between media firms and advertisers; it is about the marriage of editorial/entertainment and commercialism to such an extent that they are becoming indistinguishable. Infomercials, for example, which once were Madison Avenue's tackiest contribution to commercial culture and which generated $14 billion via TV sales in 2001, increasingly resemble standard commercial entertainment programming. "Traditional advertising will not go away," an ad executive stated in 2002, but it "requires an entirely new set of creative tools." "Product placement is silly and overblown," another ad executive stated. It can only work "if it's integral to the story line." Accordingly, the largest advertising agencies have begun working aggressively to co-produce programming in conjunction with the largest media firms. In 2003, AOL Time Warner's WB network worked with advertisers on the first program without any commercial interruptions, but with advertising messages incorporated directly into the show. Produced by Michael Davies, who developed the reality show "Who Wants to Be a Millionaire," the idea is to create "a contemporary, hip Ed Sullivan show" in which singers and other entertainers will perform on a set completely dominated by a product logo, such as Pepsi, and comedy routines will be designed around particular products being sold.

Advertisers Now Produce Their Own Media

Likewise, advertising agencies and corporate marketing departments are now producing their own media, in particular glossy magazines, which are often indistinguishable from traditional commercial media. Newhouse's Conde Nast publishing house launched *Lucky*, a magazine where advertising motifs dictate the design of every editorial page, and all editorial copy is linked to specific products. "Articles, in the traditional sense, are nowhere to be found." This "custom publishing market" was valued at $1.5 billion in 2001 and has been growing at 10 percent per year; traditional commercial magazine publishing revenues dropped 11.7 percent in 2001. "These magazines are direct marketing vehicles, but they're more than that," one publishing executive stated in 2002. "They are also intended to have a look and a feel of a real magazine."

Co-opting Movies and Music

Along similar lines, firms like Microsoft and Daimler-Chrysler produced lavish film shorts (and paid for them) to be shown in theaters before feature presentations; these were meant to be regarded as entertainment with the sales pitch low key. "Eventually there will be entire channels devoted to commercials," one advertising executive predicted. "It's all just content." And, indeed, the pioneer in this regard is BMW, which launched its own 24/7 channel on DirecTV in 2002. The channel features entertainment programming based around BMW automobiles. "I'm hoping it's the tip of the iceberg," an enthusiastic DirecTV executive stated. The crucial development here follows from the logic implicit in corporate advertising. It is to give brands personality, and to "brand" that personality on our brains. All of this has precious little to do with the actual attributes of the product or service being sold. As Coca-Cola's chief marketing officer put it in 2002, when people buy a can of Coke, "they are not buying a product. They are buying the idea of the branding imagery, the emotional connection—and that is all about entertainment." As an executive working with Anheuser-Busch put it: "The idea is not about promoting a product specifically, but connecting with consumers on an emotional level." And the commercial media are joined to marketers at the hip in these endeavors. Disney, for example, has its characters provide the basis for General Mills' line of fruit snack products and it ties Nestle's Wonderball chocolate bar to its children's films, to mention just a couple.

Another key area where the merger of commercialism and content has become more and more prevalent is in recorded music, and here again the consequences are troubling. Late in 2002, for example, Pepsi and Sony Music signed a groundbreaking deal, whereby Sony artists will be promoted and distributed in many places Pepsi is sold, while Pepsi will get exclusive rights to use Sony music in its global marketing campaigns. "Music is part of our DNA," a Pepsi executive stated. "Working with Sony lets us bring it to life in the marketplace. The umbrella idea is that Pepsi is bringing you music first. It reinforces Pepsi's connection and leadership in music as a marketer at the same time it allows Sony to get airplay for artists early and often."

AOL Time Warner struck a deal with Toyota in 2002 that, among other things, called for a single from Phil Collins' new CD to be used during Toyota TV commercials for its Avalon sedan. "We are looking for new and innovative ways to get music out to the public," an AOL Time Warner executive explained. "Toyota is the most collaborative partner we ever had. This is real co-marketing." Toyota, Chrysler, and Honda all sponsor alternative music tours, "hoping to slip in some brand messages to a jaded demographic." In 2002 Chevrolet sponsored the "Come Together and Worship Tour" of evangelical Christian artists, at the same time it was the exclusive sponsor of *Rolling Stone*'s twenty-eight-page 2003 calendar insert in an issue with Eminem on the cover. . . .

A Commercial Tidal Wave

Much of the media have been commercial institutions in the United States for generations, and what we describe is simply a massive and qualitative leap in a pre-existing commercialism. Its flames are fanned by the privatization urged on by neoliberal policies. Concurrently, and every bit as important as what we have described herein, there is an ongoing privatization and commercialization of virtually all those institutions—media and otherwise—that have been decidedly and explicitly noncommercial. This includes public broadcasting, public education, art, university education, and government activities. In grand irony, even "anti-establishment" institutions like independent films, increasingly turn to explicit corporate sponsorship. As Thomas Frank and Matt Weiland [editors of the book *Commmodify Your Dissent*] put it, we are in an age when people are channeled to "commodify your dissent," with all that that suggests about the range of opinions that will be encouraged. Fittingly, "cause-related marketing," where advertisers link their product to some worthy social cause to enhance their bottom line, has boomed over the past decade. Indeed, advertising itself is far too narrow a concept to encompass the effects of the rampant commercialism that now confronts us. Much attention is devoted today to how marketing and public relations are effectively merging, as both swallow up and direct the entire culture. In this sense the commercial tidal wave is interchangeable with a broader media torrent, or blizzard, that overwhelms our senses. The culture it generates tends to be more depoliticized, garish, and vulgar than what it has replaced.

Periodical Bibliography

The following articles have been selected to supplement the diverse views presented in this chapter.

Stephen Baker	"The Online Ad Surge," *Business Week*, November 22, 2004.
Melissa Campanelli	"Once You Pop," *Entrepreneur*, June 2002.
Jay Chiat	"How Will Advertising Reach Us?" *Time*, May 22, 2000.
Current Events	"On with the Show?" April 25, 2003.
Nick Dager	"Signage in the Brave New World," *Digital Video Magazine*, October 1, 2004.
Chris Dillabough	"Industry Must Unite to Stop Growth of a Pop-up Plague," *New Media Age*, August 15, 2002.
Michele Orecklin	"There's No Escape," *Time*, May 5, 2003.
Jim Rapoza	"Pop-up Ads," *eWeek*, March 8, 2004.
Tom Spring	"Spam Wars Rage," *PC World*, April 2004.
Gregory Wilson	"The Un-Massing of the Mass Media," *Shoot*, September 5, 2003.
Louise Witt	"Inside Intent," *American Demographics*, March 1, 2004.
Michael Zuzel	"Is 'Spam' Overflowing?" *Masthead*, Winter 2003.

For Further Discussion

Chapter 1

1. After reading the viewpoints in this chapter, do you believe the effects of advertising are largely positive or negative? What do you feel is the most significant way that advertising affects society? Explain your answers.

2. The viewpoints on male and female stereotypes are both coauthored by women. If you agree with the views expressed by Ivy McClure Stewart and Kate Kennedy, do you believe that women are better suited to provide an unbiased analysis of male roles in commercials than a male author could? On the other hand, if you support Katherine Toland Frith and Barbara Mueller's conclusions, do you think that women can recognize antifemale stereotypes that men cannot? How would your opinions change if these viewpoints had been written by men? Explain your answers.

3. Tom Reichert contends that advertisements that use sexual innuendo are highly effective among teenagers and young adults. As a member of that demographic, do you agree with his conclusions? Why or why not?

Chapter 2

1. Several of the viewpoints in this chapter maintain that ads have a significant effect on adolescent behavior and suggest that business and government should develop solutions to reduce this influence. Do you believe that advertising has a negative influence? If so, do you agree with the solutions offered by the authors? Why or why not? If you believe that advertising is not harmful to children, detail some of its benefits.

2. After reading the viewpoints by Alex Molnar and William C. Bosher Jr., Kate R. Kaminski, and Richard S. Vacca, and taking into account your personal experiences with advertising in schools, do you believe that such advertising is harmful or helpful to students? Explain your answer.

3. Jacob Sullum argues that the Center on Alcohol Marketing and Youth's 2002 report on alcohol commercials is banal and illogical. Do you agree with his assessment? Why or why not? Furthermore, how do you think Sullum would respond to the April 2004 CAMY report that appeared in this chapter?

Chapter 3

1. After reading the viewpoints in this chapter, which reforms do you believe would have the most positive effect on political advertis-

ing? Are there other remedies that were not discussed that you believe would be more beneficial? Please explain your answers.

2. David Limbaugh contends that negative political ads can provide voters with important information. However, he does not offer ways to ensure that those commercials are truthful. Meanwhile, Timothy Karr suggests that television journalists should verify the content of negative advertisements. Do you think fact checking political ads is the responsibility of the news media, or is it up to voters to determine for themselves whether a political ad is telling the truth? Explain your answers.

3. Trevor Potter and Robert J. Samuelson disagree on the constitutionality of campaign-finance reform laws. Whose argument do you find more convincing and why? If you think such laws are not constitutional, do you believe that there can be acceptable limits to political free speech or are any such restrictions harmful to the political process? Please explain your answers.

Chapter 4

1. After reading the viewpoints in this chapter, and considering your personal experiences, do you feel that advertising has become too ubiquitous? What types of ads do you believe are the most invasive? Please explain your answers.

2. In her viewpoint Wendy M. Grossman offers several ways to reduce spam. She suggests that community efforts will be most effective. Do you agree with that assessment, or do you feel that the other solutions she described would be more beneficial? Explain your answers.

3. Robert W. McChesney and John Bellamy Foster are editors for a magazine that is critical of capitalism. How does this affect your response to their viewpoint? Would you find a viewpoint on the pervasiveness of advertising more compelling if it had been written by someone in the industry? Why or why not?

Organizations to Contact

The editors have compiled the following list of organizations concerned with the issues debated in this book. The descriptions are derived from materials provided by the organizations. All have publications or information available for interested readers. The list was compiled on the date of publication of the present volume; the information provided here may change. Be aware that many organizations take several weeks or longer to respond to inquiries, so allow as much time as possible.

Adbusters Media Foundation
1234 West Seventh Ave., Vancouver, BC V6H 1B7 Canada
(604) 736-9401 • fax: (604) 737-6021
e-mail: info@adbusters.org • Web site: www.adbusters.org

Adbusters is a network of artists, activists, writers, and other people who want to build a new social activist movement. The organization publishes *Adbusters* magazine, which explores the ways that commercialism destroys physical and cultural environments. Spoof ads and information on political action are available on the Web site.

Ad Council
261 Madison Ave., 11th Fl., New York, NY 10016
(212) 922-1500 • fax: (212) 922-1676
e-mail: info@adcouncil.org • Web site: www.adcouncil.org

The Ad Council is a nonprofit organization that works with businesses, advertisers, the media, and other nonprofit groups to produce and distribute public service campaigns. The council also conducts research in order to improve the effectiveness of its campaigns. Several research studies can be found on the Web site.

Advertising Standards Canada (ASC)
175 Bloor St. East, South Tower,
Suite 1801, Toronto, ON M4W 3R8 Canada
(416) 961-6311 • fax: (416) 961-7904
e-mail: info@adstandards.com • Web site: www.adstandards.com

Advertising Standards Canada is an organization that has more than 170 corporate members, including advertising agencies and media. ASC promotes the use of industry self-regulation as a way to ensure the integrity of advertising. The Canadian Code of Advertising Standards and links to advertising industry associations and self-regulatory bodies can be found on the site.

Association of National Advertisers (ANA)
708 Third Ave., New York, NY 10017-4270
(212) 697-5950 • fax: (212) 661-8057
Web site: www.ana.net

The Association of National Advertisers is a trade association that offers resources and training to the advertising industry. Its members provide services and products to more than three hundred companies that combined spend more than $100 billion on advertising and marketing. The association publishes the magazine *Advertiser* six times each year, and books are available for sale on its Web site.

Campaign Legal Center
1640 Rhode Island Ave. NW, Suite 650, Washington, DC 20036
(202) 736-2200 • fax: (202) 736-2222
e-mail: info@campaignlegalcenter.org
Web site: www.campaignlegalcenter.org

The Campaign Legal Center is a nonprofit and nonpartisan organization that represents the public interest in issues relating to campaign-finance and associated media laws. The center also develops legal and policy debate on political advertising. The Web site features articles and weekly reports.

Center for a New American Dream
6930 Carroll Ave., Suite 900, Takoma Park, MD 20912
(301) 891-3683 • (877) 68-DREAM
e-mail: newdream@newdream.org
Web site: www.newdream.org

The Center for a New American Dream is an organization whose goal is to help Americans consume responsibly and thus protect the earth's resources and improve quality of life. Its Kids and Commercialism Campaign provides information on the effects of advertising on children. The center publishes booklets and a quarterly newsletter, *Enough!*

Center on Alcohol Marketing and Youth (CAMY)
2233 Wisconsin Ave. NW, Suite 525, Washington, DC 20007
(202) 687-1019
e-mail: info@camy.org • Web site: www.camy.org

Based at Georgetown University, the Center on Alcohol Marketing and Youth focuses attention on the marketing practices of the alcohol industry, in particular those that may cause harm to America's youth. The Web site features numerous reports and fact sheets on alcohol advertising and the consequences of underage drinking, including *Clicking with Kids: Alcohol Marketing and Youth on the Internet* and *Overexposed: Youth a Target of Alcohol Advertising in Magazines.*

Children's Advertising Review Unit (CARU)
70 West Thirty-sixth St., 13th Fl., New York, NY 10018
(866) 334-6272 (ext. 111)
e-mail: caru@caru.bbb.org • Web site: www.caru.org

As the children's branch of the U.S. advertising industry's self-regulation program, the Children's Advertising Review Unit reviews ads aimed at children and promotes responsible children's advertising. It also corrects misleading or inaccurate commercials with the help of advertisers. Commentary and articles are available on the Web site.

Commercial Alert
4110 SE Hawthorne Blvd., #123, Portland, OR 97214
(503) 235-8012 • fax: (503) 235-5073
e-mail: info@commercialalert.org
Web site: www.commercialalert.org

Commercial Alert is a nonprofit organization whose goal is to prevent commercial culture from exploiting children and destroying family and community values. It works toward that goal by conducting campaigns against commercialism in classrooms and marketing to children. News and opportunities to take action against various marketing tactics are posted on the Web site.

Commercialism in Education Research Unit (CERU)
Box 872411, Arizona State University, Tempe, AZ 85287-2411
(480) 965-1886 • fax: (480) 965-0303
e-mail: epsl@asu.edu • Web site: www.asu.edu

The Commercialism in Education Research Unit conducts research and distributes information about commercial activities in schools. CERU also seeks to encourage dialogue among the public, the education community, and policy makers. Information available on the Web site includes an annual report and other reports, links to articles, and information on relevant legislation and litigation.

Federal Trade Commission—Bureau of Consumer Protection
600 Pennsylvania Ave. NW, Washington, DC 20580
(202) 326-2222
Web site: www.ftc.gov

Part of the Federal Trade Commission, the Bureau of Consumer Protection defends consumers against fraudulent or destructive practices. The bureau's Division of Advertising Practices protects people from deceptive advertising by monitoring advertisements for numerous products, including tobacco, alcohol, and over-the-counter drugs.

Media Awareness Network
1500 Merivale Rd., 3rd Fl., Ottawa, ON K2E 6Z5 Canada
(613) 224-7721 • fax: (613) 224-1958
e-mail: info@media-awareness.ca
Web site: www.media-awareness.ca

The Media Awareness Network is a nonprofit organization that promotes media education and develops media literacy programs. Its Media Issues section examines topics such as marketing to children and stereotyping in advertisements. The Web site also provides information for parents and educators.

Web Sites

Advertising
e-mail: advertising.guide@about.com
Web site: http://advertising.about.com

Part of the About.com collection of Web sites, this site features articles and news on advertising, professional resources, and online forums.

MediaChannel.org
575 Eighth Ave., New York, NY 10018
(212) 246-0202 • fax: (212) 246-2677
e-mail: info@mediachannel.org
Web site: www.mediachannel.org

MediaChannel.org is a nonprofit Web site that explores global media issues. In addition to news, commentaries, reports, and discussion forums, the site also provides articles on political advertising, marketing to children, and the advertising industry.

Bibliography of Books

| Richard Adams | *www.advertising.* New York: Watson-Guptill, 2003. |

Neil M. Alperstein — *Advertising in Everyday Life.* Cresskill, NJ: Hampton Press, 2003.

Arthur Asa Berger — *Ads, Fads, and Consumer Culture: Advertising's Impact on American Character and Society.* Lanham, MD: Rowman & Littlefield, 2004.

Warren Berger — *Advertising Today.* London: Phaidon, 2001.

Joe Cappo — *The Future of Advertising: New Media, New Clients, New Consumers in the Post-Television Age.* Chicago: McGraw-Hill, 2003.

Katherine Toland Frith and Barbara Mueller — *Advertising and Societies: Global Issues.* New York: Peter Lang, 2003.

Bob Garfield — *And Now a Few Words from Me: Advertising's Leading Critic Lays Down the Law, Once and for All.* New York: McGraw-Hill, 2003.

Kenneth M. Goldstein and Patricia Strach, eds. — *The Medium and the Message: Television Advertising and American Elections.* Upper Saddle River, NJ: Pearson/Prentice-Hall, 2004.

Shari Graydon — *Made You Look: How Advertising Works and Why You Should Know.* New York: Annick Press, 2003.

Barrie Gunter — *Advertising to Children on TV: Content, Impact, and Regulation.* Mahwah, NJ: Lawrence Erlbaum, 2005.

Carl Hausman — *Lies We Live By: Defeating Double-Talk and Deception in Advertising, Politics, and the Media.* New York: Routledge, 2000.

Daniel D. Hill — *Advertising to the American Woman, 1900–1999.* Columbus: Ohio State University Press, 2002.

Barry Hoffman — *The Fine Art of Advertising: Irreverent, Irrepressible, Irresistibly Ironic.* New York: Stewart, Tabori & Chang, 2002.

John Philip Jones — *The Ultimate Secrets of Advertising.* Thousand Oaks, CA: Sage Publications, 2002.

John Philip Jones, ed. — *International Advertising: Realities and Myths.* Thousand Oaks, CA: Sage Publications, 2000.

Barbara K. Kaye and Norman J. Medoff — *Just a Click Away: Advertising on the Internet.* Boston: Allyn and Bacon, 2001.

Thomas J. Kuegler — *Web Advertising and Marketing.* Roseville, CA: Prima Tech, 2000.

Martin Lindstrom

Brandchild: Remarkable Insights into the Minds of Today's Global Kids and Their Relationships with Brands. London: Kogan Page, 2003.

Susan E. Linn

Consuming Kids: The Hostile Takeover of Childhood. New York: New Press, 2004.

Barton Macchiette and Abhijit Roy, eds.

Taking Sides: Clashing Views on Controversial Issues in Marketing. Guilford, CT: McGraw-Hill/Dushkin, 2001.

Tom Reichert

The Erotic History of Advertising. Amherst, NY: Prometheus Books, 2003.

Tom Reichert and Jacqueline Lambiase, eds.

Sex in Advertising: Perspectives on the Erotic Appeal. Mahwah, NJ: Lawrence Erlbaum, 2003.

Glenn W. Richardson

Pulp Politics: How Political Advertising Tells the Stories of American Politics. Lanham, MD: Rowman & Littlefield, 2003.

Al Ries and Laura Ries

The Fall of Advertising and the Rise of PR. New York: HarperBusiness, 2002.

Lawrence R. Samuel

Brought to You By: Postwar Television Advertising and the American Dream. Austin: University of Texas Press, 2001.

Juliet Schor

Born to Buy: The Commercialized Child and the New Consumer Culture. New York: Scribner, 2004.

Gerard J. Tellis

Effective Advertising: Understanding When, How, and Why Advertising Works. Thousand Oaks, CA: Sage Publications, 2004.

James B. Twitchell

20 Ads That Shook the World: The Century's Most Groundbreaking Advertising and How It Changed Us All. New York: Three Rivers Press, 2000.

Jan Zimmerman

Marketing on the Internet. Gulf Breeze, FL: Maximum Press, 2000.

Peter Zollo

Getting Wiser to Teens: More Insights into Marketing to Teenagers. Ithaca, NY: New Strategist, 2004.

Index